ACHIEVING
BUSINESS VALUE
FROM TECHNOLOGY

Achieving Business Value from Technology

A Practical Guide for Today's Executive

TONY MURPHY

gartnerpress

JOHN WILEY & SONS, INC.

For general information on our other products and services please contact our Customer Care Department within the U.S. at (800) 762-2974, outside the United States at (317) 572-3993 or fax (317) 572-4002.

Wiley also publishes its books in a variety of electronic formats. Some content that appears in print may not be available in electronic books. For more information about Wiley products visit our Web site at www.wiley.com.

ISBN 0-471-23230-0

Printed in the United States of America.

10 9 8 7 6 5 4 3 2

Acknowledgments

Over many years, I have been privileged to work with a group of enormously talented and dedicated professionals, both among colleagues and clients. I believe that this exposure has contributed significantly to this book, not least in terms of its being practical and applicable. I owe a special debt to my colleagues in Gartner's Cork office, who identified new and innovative ways in which the framework could be applied. They encouraged me to build on and extend what was originally my PhD thesis into a practical tool for business users. I must confess that at the time I did not share their faith in its potential. I have also leaned heavily on Gartner's unparalleled research resources, facilities, and the company's thought-leaders in this field such as Tim Ogden, who made a huge contribution to the book's structure, and Bill Kirwin, who really kicked the whole project off. Finally, I want to express particular gratitude to Michael (Mick) Loftus. Mick is no longer with Gartner, having "retired" to academia, but nonetheless contributed hugely not just to this book, but in terms of structuring and putting "shape" on the whole framework.

Contents

Introduction

The past few years have produced a confluence of events that have reshaped the global economy. Around the world, free-market competition has flourished and a new globally interdependent financial system has emerged. Whatever we might think about it as individuals, and despite very vocal opposition, the system is likely to remain. Reflecting these changes, core business relationships and models are dramatically changing, including shifts from:

- ➤ Product centricity to customer centricity.
- ➤ Mass production to mass customization.
- ➤ Protracted value chains to speed-based competition.
- ➤ Traditional employment arrangements to the growth of free agency.
- ➤ The value in material things to the value of knowledge and intelligence.

In concert with these trends, a new series of business success factors and challenges have emerged that are helping to determine marketplace winners and losers:

- ➤ Enterprise agility, often supported by a "plug and play" IT infrastructure (with a flexible and adaptable applications architecture).
- ➤ A focus on core competencies and processes.
- ➤ A redefinition of the value chain.

➤ Instantaneous business response and zero latency.

➤ the ability to scale resources and infrastructure across geographic boundaries.

Never before have IT investments played such a critical role in business success. As we enter the new millennium and as e-business strategies continue to evolve, the ability to separate "the business" from IT will become virtually impossible to accomplish. Some of the main drivers are detailed in Figure I.1.

These developments add up to an environment that is vastly more complex than even five years ago. This in turn has resulted in enterprises increasingly embracing new business models, such as the virtual enterprise. This model involves trading partners performing key activities in a tightly synchronized fashion and assuming much of the risk of bringing products and services to market. These forces require enterprises to become more externally focused in their business processes and integration architectures. This form of virtually integrated business model will cause a sharp increase in the number of business partners, and the closeness of integration

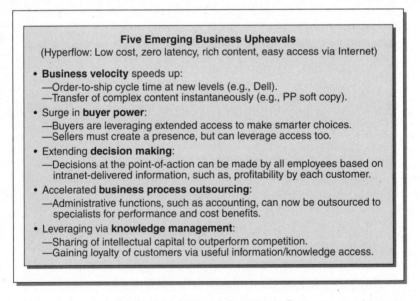

Five Emerging Business Upheavals
(Hyperflow: Low cost, zero latency, rich content, easy access via Internet)

• **Business velocity** speeds up:
  —Order-to-ship cycle time at new levels (e.g., Dell).
  —Transfer of complex content instantaneously (e.g., PP soft copy).

• Surge in **buyer power**:
  —Buyers are leveraging extended access to make smarter choices.
  —Sellers must create a presence, but can leverage access too.

• Extending **decision making**:
  —Decisions at the point-of-action can be made by all employees based on intranet-delivered information, such as, profitability by each customer.

• Accelerated **business process outsourcing**:
  —Administrative functions, such as accounting, can now be outsourced to specialists for performance and cost benefits.

• Leveraging via **knowledge management**:
  —Sharing of intellectual capital to outperform competition.
  —Gaining loyalty of customers via useful information/knowledge access.

Figure I.1 Information Hyperflow

between them. For this new model to perform to specification, partner companies will need to share not only data types, but also the meanings of all relevant data, and the fundamentals of their business processes.

In addition, each enterprise becomes a "virtual employer" for all employees in the "ecosystem." This makes it more difficult than ever for collaborating knowledge workers—who act across company boundaries—to understand their roles and to support virtual enterprise's goals.

These developments, supported by decreasing unit costs of basic technologies (e.g., processors, storage, bandwidth), have transformed IT. IT has rapidly expanded from a backroom resource providing competitive advantage (e.g., cost, time, quality) to a front-office resource (e.g., marketing, sales, environmental scan) that is a competitive necessity. New technologies have arisen to support these developments. But these new technologies have themselves acted as catalysts for new competitive initiatives, which in turn generate new critical success factors for IT investment. It is these factors that will drive business value from IT. The need to operate in a dynamic business and technical environment is driving the need for technology infrastructures and application architectures that are increasingly more flexible, integrated and maintainable (while still providing functionality, cost effectiveness and a timely and secure environment).

While Internet and Web technologies would obviously spring to mind, today's executives must understand the impact (not the technologies themselves) of a bewildering range of new technologies such as:

➤ Customer relationship management (CRM).

➤ Middleware and systems integration tools.

➤ Computer/telephone integration (CTI).

➤ The transition from Enterprise Resource Planning (ERP) applications to ERP II.

➤ Convergence in electronic messaging (e-mail, groupware, workflow).

➤ Device proliferation and supporting technologies.

To add to the complexity, executives have to wrestle with these challenges in the context of heavy investment in legacy applications.

These developments have, not surprisingly, been paralleled by continuing rapid growth in IT expenditure, as indicated in Figure I.2. In the United States alone, annual expenditure now runs into trillions of dollars, and approaches 50 percent of new capital investment for most organizations. While many individual initiatives have generated tremendous payback in terms of effectiveness and enhanced competitiveness, there is regrettably little evidence to suggest that this expenditure has in an overall macro sense generated a satisfactory return. The

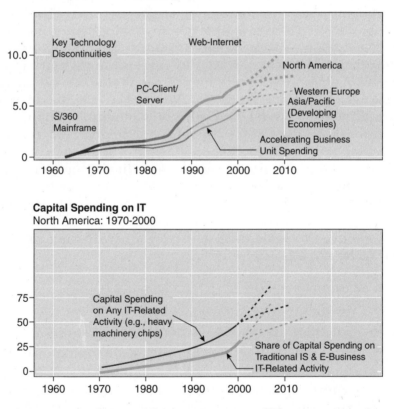

Figure I.2 Total IT Spending as a Percentage of Revenue: Central IS Combined with Business Unit IT Spending

corollary of this is that individual organizations overall have not achieved the appropriate productivity improvements. Underlining this interpretation, if IT investments improve productivity, those industries making the most-intensive use of IT should show higher productivity growth than industries that use IT less intensively.

Yet, evidence of such a pattern at industry level remains mixed at best: Official output measures for IT-intensive service industries actually indicate declining productivity in 1990–1997, while some research actually shows a negative relationship between IT spend and corporate performance in some cases. In other words, the more you spend on IT, the worse your performance!

At first glance, this must appear as a dreadful indictment of IT. However, such disappointing results have accompanied the introduction of most breakthrough technological advances. There is always a period of experimentation and exploration, as people struggle to adapt to new ways of working and doing business. This is then followed by the productive phase. This has already happened in many areas of IT (e.g., the automating of routine tasks) and will in due course extend even further. So the key objective for every enterprise today is to shorten the time it takes to achieve effective acquisition and deployment. In the light of these developments, business and IT executives must make informed decisions, and answer the following questions:

- ➤ How can we identify those projects with the highest potential business returns?
- ➤ How do we best convince senior executives or shareholders that we have a practical approach to achieving business benefits from IT investments?
- ➤ Are there any techniques that help put harder numbers on intangible benefits?
- ➤ Can we be sure that the anticipated benefits will be realized?
- ➤ How do we reconcile and integrate individual IT projects with other projects (both business and IT)?

➤ What should we do if an IT project looks unlikely to meet the original objectives?

➤ What happens to the original justification when a project gets overtaken by changes in the business or technology environments?

While these are difficult challenges, they can be overcome. But there is no silver bullet. The solution calls for active and ongoing commitment not only from IT, but also from business managers throughout the organization. The good news is that there are proven techniques, methodologies, governance mechanisms, and best practice guidelines to meet this challenge. This book provides one such approach that has been successfully applied in a wide range of organizations over a period of six years.

We start by putting the issues in context and also look at a little "history" to see how we have arrived at the present set of challenges. This is important because it provides an understanding of the foundations on which the suggestions that follow can most effectively be implemented. This section shows, inter alia, that many of the difficulties in achieving benefits stem from a failure to take a number of decisive factors into account. These factors (or perspectives, as we prefer to call them) and the way in which they are embodied in the decision-making process, are central to our approach. We will take a detailed look at how these perspectives can be identified, classified and prioritized by the investment team, and then provide a governance structure (i.e., roles, responsibilities, accountabilities) which optimizes the opportunities for success.

We will also provide best practice guidelines for quantifying benefits, undertaking postimplementation benefits audits (both much neglected areas), and IT sourcing, together with tips and techniques for optimizing asset management and minimizing ongoing total cost of ownership (TCO).

The objectives therefore in producing this book are to:

1. Address a weakness present in most management systems today—the absence of a systematic process to identify,

track, and realize the benefits from IT investments, and thereby derive business value from IT investments.

2. Provide management with a language that helps bridge the business/IT chasm and that enables its metrics to be incorporated into conventional management reporting systems.

3. Clarify the cause and effect relationships of investments and benefits, and monitor opportunities, risks, and impediments at all stages of the investment cycle.

4. Enable individuals and departments to understand how the various components of our approach hang together, and how their actions can contribute to successful investments.

5. Provide a strategic learning framework whereby every iteration adds to the store of corporate knowledge and management understanding of IT cost/benefit dynamics. This process is taken a step further by incorporating double-loop learning rather than single-loop learning. Single-loop learning, the conventional approach, seeks to establish the extent to which existing plans and strategies are being met. Double-loop learning takes this a step further by continually opening to question whether these strategies and plans continue to be valid in the light of changes in the business and/or technology arenas.

6. Present an approach that sees measures and accountabilities as a learning mechanism, keeping staff focused on supporting business objectives and strategies. This contrasts with conventional methods that focus on the past to control future behavior.

This book opens up new territory in terms of achieving business value from IT (BVIT), and BVIT will be fundamental to the ongoing success of your organization. While not the only "solution" in this space, if used as recommended, it will become a valuable tool for ongoing management of your IT portfolio.

Chapter 1

Industrial Age Thinking for Information Age Problems

"No more investment unless there's a direct financial benefit."

Thus, an exasperated finance director or CFO (let's call him James) reacted to a seemingly endless stream of requests for enhancements to the comprehensive Enterprise Resource Planning (ERP) application which, he had been assured, would solve all of his problems. The results of these incessant requests were major cost over-runs and worse, from James' perspective, long delays in getting the system operational. It seemed as if he was signing an endless stream of checks and he had no idea what he was getting in return. Operating in the highly competitive retail sector, his company could ill afford the delays, errors, and customer dissatisfaction stemming from his system's problems.

He was obviously worried, but also felt somewhat "betrayed," as he described it. "We did everything possible," he complained, "brought in consultants to help us, did a detailed definition of requirements, spent months evaluating vendor responses, visited reference sites, paid top dollar for the application, and gave the users comprehensive training. What more could we have done?" What more indeed? We'll return to this shortly. James had to face what untold numbers of business and information technology (IT) executives had faced before, are facing now, and will face again.

■ BUSINESS VALUE FROM INFORMATION TECHNOLOGY (BVIT)—A LARGE AND GROWING PROBLEM

Obtaining business value from IT investments continues to be among the top concerns of CIOs and CEOs, as evidenced by Gartner's annual survey of business and information technology executives. As they approve large and ever-growing expenditures on IT initiatives, executives are unsure when, or even if, there will be a return on these investments. Should they even briefly examine some relevant research findings, their confidence would be even further undermined. For instance, the research by Paul Strassman (one of the leading authorities in this area) shows no correlation between investment in IT and the overall performance of the firm. In other words, high spenders on IT did no better than those that spent comparatively little and, in case you are wondering, Strassman was careful to compare like with like (e.g., sector, size, location). One study by the Massachusetts Institute of Technology was even worse; it showed a negative return, that is, the more a firm spent on IT, the worse it did! Later, we'll see numerous examples of outstandingly successful IT deployments. What makes the difference?

In terms of failed projects (let's not address just what constitutes a failed project for the moment), different studies have suggested that the cost of such projects have to-date amounted to close to $200 billion in the United States alone. That is not only in terms of direct financial impact. Think of the business disruption that was endured in vain, the competitive opportunities missed, and the disillusionment in IT that such failures occasioned.

Despite all of this, we know that IT has also produced tremendous benefits. Automation in manufacturing has sharply reduced cost and lead times while increasing quality. Armies of paper-shuffling clerks have been released to perform higher value-adding activities (or have been fired!) by the deployment of technologies such as workflow while airlines, financial services, and telephone companies (telcos) are wholly dependent on IT for their core transaction processing functions. On a more modest scale, individual users or business departments have used a variety of productivity tools to enhance and enrich their performances and operating environments.

Looking at the issue from another perspective, the poor returns from IT should not come as too much of a surprise. The introduction of breakthrough initiatives has historically taken a very long time to provide a return on investment (ROI). For example, after Edison's deployment of the first dynamo in New York in 1881 (the first industrial use of electricity), tangible productivity improvements did not emerge until the 1920s. An even longer productivity delay (about 50 years) followed the introduction of Watt's steam engine in the late eighteenth century. Similar delays were experienced with investments in railroads. Benefits don't occur until the technology matures and society has had sufficient opportunity to adapt to them. While it would be dangerous to make a direct comparison to IT, there is little doubt that businesses and society are struggling to adapt work patterns and processes. This suggests that those organizations that do manage to adapt will gain greater returns. The framework developed as we go through this book is one way of achieving these elusive returns *ahead of the curve*.

■ LEARNING FROM CASE STUDIES

What is the explanation? On the basis that we can learn more from our failures than our successes, let's look at some case studies of failed investments. we'll repeatedly return to these case studies to illustrate developments as we go through the book; please give them careful attention. To help you remember, I'll assign each one a name.

➤ Heavy Manufacturing Enterprise

Having sustained heavy losses for a number of years, this company was undergoing a program of radical change, led by a new CEO. In his view, the enterprise's manufacturing operations had grown flabby and inefficient while its product line had not changed significantly for many years. He saw an immediate opportunity to increase sales by selling product at a number of intermediate stages of production rather than as finished goods, as had been the case heretofore.

As can be imagined, this initiative had IT implications. Among the more significant were the need to capture production costs at the relevant production stages, accommodate a new wholesale sales network, implement structural alterations to the general ledger, and manage more complex inventory control facilities. Although the CEO wanted quick results, a detailed definition of requirements was undertaken and reputable software developers were commissioned to begin the project. While some cost and time over-runs were incurred, the project basically met its goals. The Intermediate Product System (IPS) proved to be stable and secure, and provided accurate data and handling facilities that enabled new and profitable markets to be opened.

Sounds like a rare and unqualified success? Well, yes and no. By achieving the stated objectives, it was successful, but wider issues had not been considered at the time the project had been commissioned and these had a devastating impact on the investment. The enterprise's core transaction processing and finance systems were very old (about 10 years in operation) and both the operating system and hardware were of the same vintage. It was increasingly difficult and costly to maintain both the applications and the systems environment. But even worse for the CEO as he drove his transformation vision forward, it became increasingly clear that this environment was acting as an impediment, both in terms of flexibility and scalability. This is understandable when you realize that Customer Relationship Management (CRM), workflow, and supply chain integration were among the applications envisioned. All of these impose heavy demands on the IT infrastructure, call for close systems integration, and place heavy requirements for flexibility in the architecture.

There was no alternative but to fundamentally redesign the IT operational and application environment to support these objectives. The problem was that the Intermediate Product

System had been written to integrate closely with the existing applications and to run on existing platforms. Because of this, a virtually total rewrite would now be required—and it had been in operation for only a little more than 12 months! There was another problem. To speed up operations and to reduce errors (both had historically been major problem areas in this firm), every step of the intermediate product production and distribution process had been embedded in the software. The system called for a rigid set of activities to be performed throughout the process, and in strict order—in other words, the business process had been embedded in the software. While the stated objectives of speed and accuracy had been achieved, the CEO saw flexibility in work practices and business processes as essential to the corporate transformation exercise. In the first year or so of the system's operation, its inflexibility had little impact, but as business process redesign went into effect, it became clear that the Intermediate Product System was a major stumbling block. "The system won't allow us to do it any other way," became a common response from stakeholders, to the CEO's exasperation.

So, the IPS investment had to be written off after little more than a year in operation, and the required functionality was incorporated into a new set of integrated packaged applications running on an updated infrastructure. This occurrence we refer to as *benefits leakage*. As Figure 1.1 illustrates, projects often show an initial surge in value that tails off due to inadequate investment appraisal or benefits realization.

Let's refer to this case as *The Gung-Ho CEO*.

➤ Banking Corporation (1)

This bank had undergone structural change, most of it driven by technology and increased competition. Management now wanted to increase the number and value of the products each customer maintained with the institution. To do so, they needed to base their sales and marketing efforts on each prospect's individual behavior and activities. Like many other enterprises in this sector, the bank had no unified view of the customer and poor insight into key trends and patterns.

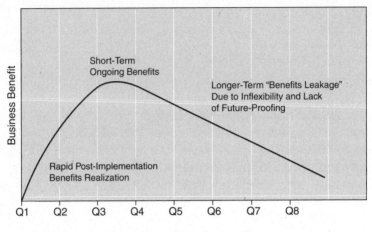

Figure 1.1 Benefits Leakage

Management saw the solution in the form of a data warehouse that would harvest, store, and disseminate the rich repositories of transaction data each customer generated. Marketing and pricing strategies would then be modified to accommodate the value contribution of key customer segments. A cost/benefit analysis was undertaken, and a clear ROI was identified.

A team composed mainly of marketing and IT members undertook a detailed study of the available alternatives. This was a high-level and well-resourced team that understood the key success factors in selecting and implementing a data warehouse. These factors included systems integration and performance, but also softer ones such as data ownership conflicts, process redesign requirements, and uneven contribution from different business units. After a thorough exercise lasting about eight months, the team recommended a solution based on two physical warehouses under one logical model. These are the strengths and weaknesses that determined the trade-off:

Strengths

➤ Allowed analysis between the business units.

➤ Provided a consistent set of data warehousing tools.

➤ Allowed independent implementation in coordination with each department's strategic needs.

➤ Shared analytics by business units to obtain a single baseline set of reports.

➤ Served as a stepping-stone to combine marketing programs.

Weaknesses

➤ Implementation would be more costly and complex than a single warehouse.

➤ Coordination between business units would be required for extension or enhancement.

Top management accepted the ROI calculations, gave approval for the project, and implementation began. Everybody got to work: extracting, cleansing, and normalizing data; putting the hardware and software in place; agreeing on analytics, and so on. However, a few months into the project, the enterprise's Board made an announcement that would have a devastating impact on the project. The Board announced it was in negotiations to take over another bank. The target's technical infrastructure, their data structures, the significantly increased data requirements plus a range of soft factors meant that the project had to be put on hold. In due course, it virtually had to be abandoned and a whole new integration exercise commenced.

We'll call this case *The Secretive Bank*.

➤ Banking Corporation (2)

In 1997, a regional bank in the United States that was fresh from a round of mergers looked to a data warehouse to provide more focused analyses of its most profitable customers with highly personalized direct-marketing campaigns. Prior to the implementation, this financial institution reorganized into four main market areas:

1. Retail and community banking.
2. Corporate banking.
3. Investments.
4. Consumer finance.

This reorganization provided a way to break down several business empires based on products and encourage the sharing of information across products. Different product groups and individual sales representatives were designing independent marketing campaigns that, in many cases, competed for the same customers as the bank. These campaigns were designed with gut-feel intuition and little hard data. The result was that the bank saw its profitability per customer decline and lag behind that of the industry leaders. To address the problem, the executive management team initiated a data warehouse study that indicated a clear ROI. The resultant project would gather all the information the bank possessed about its customers and prospects into a structured, accessible repository.

Data related to products, accounts, and revenue was managed in more than 40 different source databases which made it difficult to obtain data to perform analysis and support more intelligent decision making. The data warehouse implementation effort was initiated with the goal of providing support for several critical customer-driven areas of the bank including call center, finance, and marketing. Instead, the project focused on each of the specific application areas that has led this bank down the road of multiple data marts and not an application-neutral data warehouse.

Starting with a customer data warehouse to support the call center that was already in place, the second data warehouse effort focused on products and cross-selling opportunities. A third data warehouse was required to support the finance department and maintain the profitability data to be used in customer profitability analysis. Now the credit department required the deployment of a risk management application. With all the data in sight and available in the three data warehouses, the bank determined that yet another data warehouse would be required to support this new application because none of the data warehouses could accommodate the additional data without a significant architectural rework. It also decided that it would take 18 months to implement this new data warehouse which prompted staff members in the credit department to believe that the initial data warehouses were failures and not living up to expectations.

With the application-specific approach taken to build the data warehouses, this bank built several data marts designed to support specific applications. These efforts each took 18 to 24 months to implement. Such an implementation lacked the flexibility to support changes (based on user and business requirements) to the applications or to support new applications that were not considered initially. This could lead to significant opportunity loss in the future and the inability to deploy new high-profile business intelligence applications (e.g., stakeholder relationship management) that have experienced shorter business value lifecycles.

While this bank received some benefits from implementing the marketing data warehouse with improved cross-selling at significantly less cost, the dynamic nature of the financial services industry has left this bank behind. Early warning signs occurred at the start of the third data warehouse effort, with data that was already present (but not in a usable model) in the first two data warehouses. The benefits of flexibility obtained from a cross-functional, application-neutral data warehouse have eluded this bank, which led to longer application deployment time frames and a business opportunity loss.

We'll call this case *Silo Myopia*.

➤ Telecommunications Equipment Provider

This telecommunications equipment provider undertook custom work for the design and development of hardware and software components for major telcos. When this enterprise's salesforce completed a sale, they had to enter the details on a technical order form, which was then submitted to engineering/manufacturing. However, the sales staff focused more closely on winning the deal rather than entering the order details correctly. Their carelessness created many problems and inefficiencies once order processing and manufacturing started, among them production delays, cost over-runs, and lower quality. As various threats and inducements over a protracted period failed to change sales staff behavior, management decided to invest in a custom-built sales configurator application, estimating that the initial investment would be recouped in less than a year. A sales configurator deploys strong integrity and consistency checking and the chosen solution would eliminate the very problems experienced at order submission. Though the sales staff was represented on the team that developed the specifications, in practice participants from the engineering and manufacturing divisions did almost all of the work.

It was only when the users started training on the system that the problems began to appear. Users saw the application as complex and time-consuming and, more importantly, it did nothing for them. The net result was that they ensured the application wouldn't work. It was not that they refused to operate it—that would have resulted in disciplinary action—they just ensured that it became unworkable! It was eventually withdrawn, and the company is still working on a solution to the issue.

We'll call this case *Who Feels the Pain Must See the Gain.*

➤ **Sporting Goods Manufacturer**

This enterprise had a global manufacturing operation and implemented an Enterprise Resource Planning (ERP) system from a well-established vendor to address a range of requirements. These included:

➤ Gaining a consolidated financial view of worldwide operations, which were fragmented and nonintegrated due, in part, to a number of mergers and takeovers by the enterprise.

➤ Achieving major cost-savings and efficiencies through supplier management, using the ERP's purchasing, payments, and analytical modules.

➤ Achieving significant plant-level efficiencies by consolidating various islands of automation, electronic document management, and better inventory management (mainly lower carrying costs, fewer stock outages, and less obsolete product).

When Gartner was called in, the application had been operational in one of the plants for about nine months and all parties agreed that, far from improving, almost everything had gotten worse. But this was all they agreed on. Business units, the internal IT department, the implementers, and the software vendors all pointed at one another. It was always somebody else's fault. Upon analyzing the situation, we found, for the most part, all the participants had carried out their agreed roles. But the plant was operating less efficiently and, in some people's opinion, was "slowly grinding to a halt." Another strange failure, and one that had senior management extremely worried.

This case we'll know as *The ZAPped Manufacturer.*

■ WHAT DO THESE CASE STUDIES HAVE IN COMMON?

What can we learn from these case studies? All of these investments failed and for very different reasons. Yet, what's remarkable is that none of the usual suspects associated with such failures was involved. Clear cost/benefit and ROI analyzes were undertaken, and the definition of requirements was reasonably competent in each case, as was project management. The technology choices were adequate and management support (and funds) was never a problem. What went wrong?

In a sense, that question is what this book is all about. IT investments are becoming much more complex as we enter the seventh decade of IT and investment techniques that sufficed in an earlier time no longer work today. Yet, crucially, management still approaches such decisions using these old techniques. This brings us all the way back to James, our CFO in the retail sector referred to at the start of this chapter. His demand that any further modifications be justified by financial payback demonstrates the problem in a simplistic but brilliantly clear way. Industrial Age solutions for Information Age

Problems. This (and a lot more) will become clearer as we look at a little history.

■ SOME HISTORICAL PERSPECTIVE

Before suggesting an Information Age solution, we need to gain a good understanding of how this challenge evolved. As Figure 1.2 shows, Gartner sees the history of IT as divisible into four Eras.

➤ Era I: Automation, Cost Control, and Efficiency

In this phase, computers were acquired to automate specific business or organizational functions, usually those involving large volumes of repetitive transactions. Typical applications would be payroll or order processing. Individual departments would specify their requirements, which would, in turn, have been derived from goals assigned to these departments at corporate level. Systems analysts would design the systems and programmers would write the code. A vast gulf separated the IT

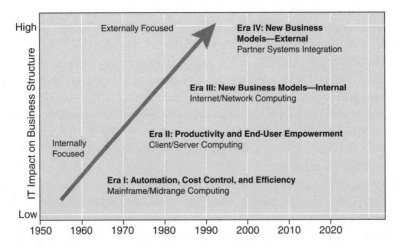

Figure 1.2 IT's Changing Destiny: Evolving IT Investment Drivers and Technology Cycles

(or Data Processing or DP, as it was known then) staff from their colleagues in the user departments. Denizens of the "glasshouse," as the computer room was often referred to, were strange creatures, best left alone. Not only was there a physical separation, but the DP staff knew virtually nothing about business issues. The users knew even less about computer matters and were not encouraged. This inevitably led to misunderstandings on both sides, but the problem was mitigated by the fact that the computer system invariably replaced its direct manual equivalent—even the forms and reports were often replicates of the manual versions. Despite the mutual incomprehension, therefore, once IT understood the mechanics of the task, the development of the resultant system was comparatively straightforward.

The systems developed during this phase were usually geared toward eliminating paper-based processing and (or, more accurately, replace paper with its computer-based equivalent) reducing headcount while increasing speed and accuracy. These factors would form the justification for each project, with the most significant factor being direct, tangible savings.

It was relatively easy to establish what could be automated and the impact of the automation in terms of savings. For instance, 20 clerks, many of whom would work overtime at peak periods, may have handled a company's payroll. Automating the process could mean that the manpower requirements might now be reduced to two clerks. The salaries, indirect labor costs (pensions, insurance, office space), and overtime payments of the 18 eliminated clerks would represent the system savings.

The corresponding costs of developing and running the resulting computer system were less rigorous. Even companies with sophisticated financial procedures usually confined costs to the direct and indirect labor expense associated with development, operations, data preparation and input, together with direct material costs such as stationery and, if applicable, punch cards. Amortizing the hardware, relating anticipated savings to opportunity cost, or evaluating in time/value terms (Internal Rate of Return, Net Present Value) were often not taken into account when cost-justifying a project during this

Era. These were indirectly addressed in some companies by the utilization of a throw factor, that is, a factor by which savings must exceed costs. In other words, a 40 percent throw factor (a common figure in my experience) would require savings of $200,000 where development and operational costs were estimated to be $140,000.

Normal standards would have applied to hardware purchases. In fact, exhaustive tests were performed on comparative hardware. Processor speeds, storage device capacity, input/output performance, and printer throughput were examined in detail, but individual application proposals were assessed in fairly basic terms. The emphasis was strongly on minimizing cost.

➤ Era II: Productivity and End-User Empowerment

This Era's most notable feature was the explosive growth in personal and distributed computing that followed the introduction of the PC by IBM in 1981. Prior to its introduction, users with dumb terminals could access computer-based data, but even the simplest tasks called for the mastery of a complex (by the standards of nontechnical staff) set of commands. Few anticipated the PC's impact—and that includes IBM! Its policy of making the operating system available on competitors' hardware meant that so-called clone manufacturers were in a position to produce machines much more cheaply than IBM. As prices plummeted, users, hardware manufacturers, software developers, and training specialists leapt on the PC bandwagon. Everyone, it seemed, was either using a PC or was in the PC business. This was understandable in view of the following:

➤ *A quantum leap in processing power:* Computer power exceeding in many ways. That of a 1960s mainframe could now be had for less than $10,000. Systems previously ruled out because of lack of capacity at the central computer facility now became feasible.

➤ *Readymade software:* Users, previously having had to endure lead times of up to a couple of years, could now buy off-the-shelf software packages, which often possessed superior functionality to those produced in-house.

➤ *Cheaper software:* The cost of software underwent a similarly radical transformation. Typically, an integrated accounting package, which may have entailed up to 10 or even 20 years to produce in-house, (in financial terms, maybe up to half a million dollars) was now available for a few thousand dollars.

➤ *User-defined systems:* Within a couple of years of the introduction of the PC, simplified application development tools, designed for inexperienced computer users, became available. Expectations were high. The cultural chasm between computer specialists and users was to be eliminated, and the days of users specifying their requirements and being continuously disappointed with the resulting systems were about to end. The plummeting costs of processing power and disk storage meant that unprofessional development techniques were more tolerable. While reality fell far short of such high expectations, a major empowerment of the user did take place.

➤ *Faster and better information:* Monthly reports, presented three weeks after the event on continuous stationery, began to look hopelessly passé in the new world of the PC. Instantaneous screen-based inquiry became the order of the day and easily used report generators enabled customized, attractive printouts to be obtained and modified without difficulty.

➤ *Staff mobility:* The almost homogeneous world of the PC created a new breed of company-independent computer operators. The hitherto crippling dependence on specialists was vastly reduced. For example, a company running one of the well-known PC-based accounting packages would find it relatively easy and inexpensive to find staff experienced in the operation of the computer and the software package.

The main change from Phase 1 in assessing project feasibility appears to have been an increased application of discounting techniques that addressed the concept of the time-value of money. In effect, this means that money is seen as having a cost, with the effect that earlier benefits and/or deferred costs should be attributed greater value than the discrete monetary amount—this is looked at in more depth later in this chapter. This could have been a reflection of the high inflation rates that applied at the time, and/or a realization that more sophisticated techniques were required. However, these failed to address some new issues that Phase 2 introduced.

For example, while the shared database referred to may have saved some time in eliminating the duplication inherent in the previous configuration, the main benefits might have related to the provision of more consistent and up-to-date data, benefits that did not lend themselves as easily to quantifiable analysis. Organizational matters, the ownership of data, faint blurring of functional boundaries, and information as a justification in its own right were identified as issues to be addressed. As a consequence, the concept of intangible benefits was introduced. I worked at Ford of Europe at this time and "intangible" was a dirty word in terms of identifying benefits. This was due mainly to the wide-scale practice using the intangible portion of the cost justification exercise as a balancing or residue figure to build to the required value case. This discrediting of the intangible concept was unfortunate, because the emerging potential for real, if nonquantifiable, organizational benefits was undermined.

➤ Era III: New Business Models—Internal

The most distinguishing feature of this Era is the transition of IT from purely transaction processing and user empowerment to becoming an enabler of new ways of doing business. There is increasing emphasis on viewing business as a series of processes that can and must be fundamentally redesigned and simplified by the imaginative application of IT. This approach is known variously as business reengineering, business process redesign (BPR), or business process transformation. Irrespective of the designation, it says that the old ways of doing business and, therefore, the old ways of applying IT, will no longer suffice.

The implications for IT applications are immense. Speed and flexibility in applications development, in the context of user empowerment, have now become paramount, which in turn means that existing legacy systems often act as a liability. The requirements of speed and flexibility call for the wide-spread application of rapid-development software tools and software re-use. The resulting applications are also likely to have a shorter life. For example, in the financial services sector, some applications may have a life span as short as a few months. This arises when enterprises seek to capitalize on brief windows of opportunity arising from legislative or fiscal developments. The twin demands of rapid development and short life span call for an appropriate underlying systems architecture, usually one very different from those in place.

Era III also calls for closer internal integration and an end to fragmented systems and islands of automation. As information became an increasingly important determinant of success, information sharing and knowledge management assumed greater significance. Straight-through processing, having a single view of the customer, and the need to respond quickly to an increasingly unpredictable business environment also increased pressure for better internal integration. This means that the organizational and technical barriers that have impeded such integration have to be substantially altered, as do long-held attitudes.

The resulting IT impact has been immense. There has been wholesale replacement of legacy systems by enterprise resource planning (ERP) applications, while the deployment of knowledge-sharing applications such as workflow, groupware, data warehouses, and knowledge-management applications grew rapidly. Era III also saw an explosion in the use of out-sourced IT services, to the extent that in many organizations the IT function became a broker of such services rather than a direct provider.

Era III brought the first real attempts at breaking away from accounting-based investment criteria. This stemmed from the growing realization of their inadequacies and what progress there was stemmed largely from academic and research institutions. Michael Porter's Value Chain Analysis was a significant contributor in that it sought, by identifying and isolating the key components of a firm's value creation process, to break away from the straightjacket of cost/benefit analysis. Even though some critics argue that Porter had only repackaged traditional value-added techniques, his work did result in IT investments being seen in a new light. One of the most influential writers of this period was Paul Strassman, who broke new ground by shifting the focus for payback from technology to organizational, cultural, and people issues.

There was little evidence of the successful application of these new techniques in a business environment. Two causes appear to predominate in explaining this. The first is that a convincing, practical methodology had not been developed at this stage. For instance, one research study cited examples of companies that had tried as many as a dozen different methods for evaluating the benefits of an office automation project with minimal success. The study also showed that almost 90 percent of executives encountered "great difficulty" in quantifying intangible benefits, while about 60 percent found that "uncertainty of benefits" made justification methods hard to apply. The net result was that while new approaches had been developed, few had been successfully applied in practice.

➤ Era IV: New Business Models—External

The forces driving new business models with an external focus include:

- ➤ Proliferation of the number of customer universes that must be satisfied.
- ➤ Proliferation of marketing and delivery channels.
- ➤ Increased emphasis on time-based competition, which is enabled by high-velocity processes and data exchange, touch-based competition, in which technology is substituted for labor when human contact is not critical.

➤ The emergence of global shop floors and virtual enterprises.

➤ The increase in outsourced relationships.

Globalization, competitive pressures, mobile computing, and Internet-enabled connections are all contributing to changes in the enterprise structure and increased cooperation between trading partners. Virtual enterprises built on dynamic strategic partnerships, outsourcing, and fluid organizational boundaries demand tremendous investment in technologies for communication, coordination, and collaboration. Enterprises are being forced to rethink their vision and transform their strategies, structure, and processes to accommodate ever-closer links with their business partners. These partners perform key activities in a tightly synchronized fashion, often filling orders and assuming much of the risk of bringing products and services to market.

These forces require enterprises to become more externally focused in their business processes and integration architectures. However, internal integration (Era III) must also be completed and maintained for this to be achieved. Because of these changes, we expect all enterprises to undergo a dramatic increase in the demand for external data and process interfaces. In many enterprises, the number of externally connected interfaces will surpass internal process integration demand. This is reflected in a Gartner strategic planning assumption that estimates by 2004, 80 percent of enterprises will have moved integration priority focus from internal integration to external integration.

Gartner expects this evolution to take the form illustrated in Figure 1.3. This changing business model will result in distinct and challenging strategies and models for external integration. Some key areas of focus include:

➤ *Trading-partner integration focus:* To increase their agility and lower their capital investment costs, many companies are embracing the vertical disintegration model. In this model, a company focuses on key core competencies and relies on trading partners

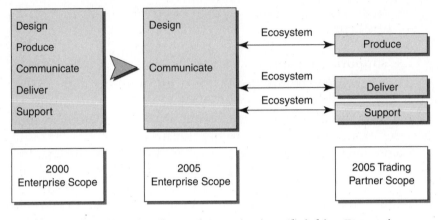

Figure 1.3   The Net-Liberated Organization: Shrinking Enterprises

for the rest. Increased outsourcing is an example of the move to vertical disintegration. Making this model work requires tight data and process-level integration with trading partners. For IS organizations, this means expanding the integration focus from integrating internal applications to include integrating external trading partners and leveraging Internet-derived technology.

Often, integration will be driven by a hub company integrating into its spoke providers to achieve tightly synchronized supply chain processes. External integration may be done through extranets, integration servers, and process ware, creating tightly coupled links for sharing real-time, event-driven information in a bi-directional business process context. EDI formats may be used to share data among trading partners, but in most cases additional forms of structured and unstructured data will also be shared.

Figure 1.3 shows how we anticipate the enterprise scope changing. Business partners increasingly undertake production, delivery, and support as part of a new ecosystem.

➤ *Value network integration focus:* Whereas the previous model is characterized by tightly coupled integration between a relatively static set of business partners, another approach is a loosely coupled integration between fluid, dynamically changing business partners. This supports plug-and-play relationships where enterprises will be able to recombine their supply chain models dynamically, based on changing customer requirements and market conditions. Technology that can enable this model includes integration hubs and Web integration servers.

In the emerging virtual world, the ability to plug in (and link) new business partners, suppliers, customers, and business processes dynamically will be critical to maintaining global competitiveness. Enterprises will begin competing with one another, not just on the products and services they provide, but also on their business models. Enterprises that can rapidly configure new business models based on changing market dynamics will have a distinct advantage over enterprises lacking the technical and business process ability to alter business models on the fly. For instance, if a customer wants product A, a process may be automatically triggered with suppliers X, Y, and Z. Moreover, the company may never have done business with supplier Z before and may never do business with it again.

We refer to this integration strategy as *consequential interoperability*—where the consequences of a business process dynamically trigger integration. Electronic marketplaces, auctions, Internet-based dynamic trading-partner communities, dynamic trading environments, and supply chain portals are enablers of this model.

Two big technical hurdles of this model are that traditional IT architectures are inflexible and difficult to integrate. Global standards for the meaning, format, and presentation of information remain a distant dream. Extensible Markup Language (XML) and some new standards initiatives (e.g., cXML, BizTalk, vertical industry groups like Rosettanet) are enabling some advances to be made.

➤ *Changing business models create IS challenges:* Enterprises that wish to participate in the emerging Internet worked economy must add a formal application interface layer to their IT architecture to build in the required flexibility for external integration and to control future integration costs. Enterprise IS organizations will be challenged not only to connect back-office systems via extranets, but also to provide flexible, secured connectivity for both long-term, strategic business relationships and short-term, opportunistic relationships.

The cultural impact of these changes is illustrated in Figure 1.4, showing the transition from hierarchical lines and boxes to a more fluid, circular structure. Also underlined are greater information democracy and the central role of the customer.

The main difference in investment appraisal techniques between Eras III and IV is that the challenge has become even more complex in the latter. The decision-making process assumes far greater complexity when trading partners are involved, especially when it is remembered that Era III is very recent and, for many firms, still with us. When the vast array of

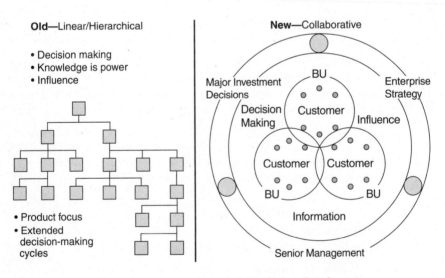

Figure 1.4 Deconstructing Traditional Culture

new technologies is added to the brew, it's not surprising that the net (no pun intended!) result is an absence of a systematic process to identify, track, and realize the benefits from IT investments and thereby derive business value from these investments. The business/IT convergence has also lead to a much greater need for a language that helps bridge the business/IT chasm and that enables its metrics to be incorporated into conventional management reporting systems. These requirements also call for governance processes to ensure that, in the event of good techniques being identified, they become institutionalized within the organization. Helping you to achieve this is the purpose of this book.

■ DRAWING CONCLUSIONS FROM THESE CHANGES

We have moved a long way in a relatively short time, although many organizations still retain Era I characteristics. A number of significant conclusions can be drawn from this evolution, all of which have a major impact on the way we handle IT investments.

➤ Sharp Growth in IT Expenditure Continues

The expenditure on IT continues to grow dramatically: The sheer speed with which IT has reshaped the global economy, challenged traditional business assumptions, and created new forms of knowledge expertise has rocked the foundation of enterprises everywhere. Gartner/Dataquest predicts that worldwide annual spending on IT will reach $1.7 trillion by 2003 ($3.2 trillion including voice communication). This spending has sharply increased over the four Eras and is likely to continue, despite the occasional downturn.

➤ Systems Integration (SI) Requirements Growing Even Faster

The demands for systems integration parallels and probably exceeds the overall growth in IT spending. This is driven by requirements within the enterprise and by business partners. This creates the network effect of adding another node—the more you automate, the more integration will be required, and it will grow geometrically rather than linearly.

➤ Larger and More Complex IT Solutions

IT solutions are expanding in range, scope, and complexity. The Internet and the Web immediately spring to mind, but other areas, including the consolidation of electronic messaging (e-mail, workflow, document management), supply chain integration, and middleware, all pose new complexity challenges.

➤ Business Processes Are Transforming

Business processes are continually changing and this change is usually enabled, if not actually driven, by IT. Business processes are also extending to trading partners, demanding even greater flexibility and responsiveness.

➤ Sourcing Practices Are Changing

Over the four Eras, the scope and scale of outsourcing have changed dramatically. Whereas initially basic operational functions such as data center and infrastructure management would have been the main functions outsourced, today many organizations outsource virtually all of the IT activities, apart from high-level strategy, and even whole business processes. This, in turn, has resulted in much more complex contractual arrangements between vendors and customers.

➤ Accountabilities for Outcomes Less Clear

All of these developments have led to diffused and unclear responsibility for outcomes. Taking a typical Era I project, the design and development of, say, a payroll application that would have been justified by the replacement of a certain number of clerks and overtime. The developers would be given a budget to bring the project on-stream. When it went live, it was expected to run in a way that replicated the functionality of the manual headcount. If the budget was exceeded, and/or if the system did not perform adequately, the responsibility was pretty clear.

Fast-forwarding to Era IV, a typical project (for example, a CRM initiative) could involve the implementation of a complex core application (e.g., Siebel or Vantive), significant systems integration (both internally and with customers), a data warehouse, computer telephony integration (CTI), redesigned business processes spanning the enterprise and its customers, plus infrastructural enhancements. If things don't work out as planned, who is accountable? Establishing such accountability has become far more complex.

➤ Death of the IT Project

The previous point suggests that there is no longer any such thing as a standalone IT project, and this is true. What we have is a variety of ongoing business initiatives supported to a greater or lesser degree by IT facilities. These initiatives do not stand alone. They often depend on one another, or even impede one another. Go back to the CRM project I referred to earlier. All the supporting technologies and process redesign initiatives could be projects in their own right, with their own full or partial justifications. But these must compete for financial funding, IT resources, and address the limitations in the organization's capacity to handle change. The sequence of implementation is also a potential problem area in that the CRM initiative might require a certain implementation sequence for each subproject. But this may not suit the proponents of these individual projects.

The common focus on IT obscures the reality that the IS organization will not operate the tools day-in, day-out once the implementation project is completed. Failure to deliver expected value will always be the IS organization's fault even though it has little control over the day-to-day operations. Business value is created through a combination of tools and business processes. The IS organization may be expert regarding the potential of IT tools, but the users are the experts on what business processes work best for them with the tools available. As such, the users must take the lead in defining how they will use the tools to achieve their business activities. This is why we say that the enterprise (and the IS organization) must view each project as a "business change project" with "IT components."

This simple change in terminology not only places the focus on those users actually able to deliver the expected value, but the project itself is viewed in its business value context. The only reason to invest in IT tools is to gain the business value expected. Proper orientation is key.

► Quantifying Benefits Is Now Much Harder

The factors that give rise to the blurring of accountabilities referred to earlier also make it much harder to quantify the benefits from IT initiatives. Going back to the payroll example of Era I, it was very simple to identify and quantify the benefits. But what about the CRM initiative of Era IV? The potential benefits from CRM are enormous. Blended sales and service call centers, interactive selling tools, customer collaboration, and tools that let customers select and configure products without direct salesperson involvement are examples of effectiveness-focused benefits, while data rationalization and CTI offer efficiency improvements.

It is difficult to establish a causal relationship between these potential benefits and the original CRM initiative. It is equally difficult to establish why anticipated benefits were not realized. Suppose that customer satisfaction had actually decreased after the project was implemented. (This is based on the major assumption that measurements to judge this would have been taken.) Customer care staff might point to overload on the network as slowing response times, and/or a data warehouse designed in a confusing manner, populated with incomplete and inaccurate data. These assertions would be disputed by the relevant technical staff who might counterclaim that lower satisfaction levels were the result of too few sales support staff and a decline in product quality. In reality, the number of variables involved in such a project would be far greater than those enumerated here, but even those few underline the difficulties.

The question is: Does this matter? Once the system is in place, let's get it working as best we can and let's not get into the blame game. This sounds reasonable, but it is a dangerous fallacy. First, it's difficult to solve a problem if you don't know what went wrong and why. Second, the opportunity for organizational learning is lost. This is a vital consideration because the same mistakes are likely to be repeated with the next project. If a project fails to deliver, it is important to understand the causes. This should be seen as a learning and corrective process rather than one of blame allocation. If projects continue to go wrong, then clearly blame lies somewhere, and the problem should be found.

➤ IT Is Now a Strategic Resource

Finally, IT has, over this evolutionary period, become a key strategic enabler. Not only an enabler, but a driver of strategic initiatives in its own right, especially in telecommunications and financial services.

While our main focus has been on business impact of IT investments, we certainly don't want to create the impression that costs don't matter. They most certainly do. Cost goes beyond just what you pay for software licenses, hardware, training, and so on. The total ongoing costs of owning an asset often exceed the original acquisition costs, yet all too often they are ignored. For this reason, we cover the concept of cost in more detail in Chapter 3.

■ REVISITING THE CASE STUDIES

In the light of these conclusions, revisiting the failed projects we referred to earlier is instructive. Remember that, in all of these initiatives, management seemed to take the right actions. There was a good business case, no significant problems related to development, implementation, or project management. Analysis will show that management used Era I methodologies for what were Era III or even Era IV projects.

➤ The Gung-Ho CEO

The first problem stemmed from addressing the business need and the related technical solution in isolation, in particular from the IT architecture. An immediate and justifiable business need was identified, but the solution ignored the longer term business and technology ramifications. This meant that the key new application was developed on an architecture that lacked scalability and the capacity to support other essential modern systems and applications. Neither was the potential impact of business change on business processes taken into account and, as we now know, this was crucial. While there was a general recognition of the need to redesign business processes, the symbiotic relationship with key underlying systems was not appreciated. The IPS was given the go ahead on the vague belief that the redesign could be done later, if this aspect was considered at all. It is much more difficult to redesign processes once they have been embedded in the software. The end result was a common syndrome, called *benefits leakage*. That is, where an initial surge of value rapidly peters out due usually to inflexibility and lack of future-proofing. This was illustrated in Figure 1.1.

➤ The Secretive Bank

In relation to the bank and the data warehouse, the problem here was undoubtedly a disconnect between high-level business planning (that is, strategy) and the IT investment process. Top management took the view that having allocated the financial and technical resources, their job was done in relation to this project apart from occasional updates on progress. But, as we saw, this disconnect undermined the rationale for the whole project.

➤ Silo Myopia

The second bank's data warehousing project also failed, but for different reasons. Here the focus was on meeting an immediate business need/opportunity, to the detriment of other aspects, or perspectives. In particular, the lack of attention given to the data and technical architecture perspectives undermined the value of the individual warehouses to such an extent that the whole exercise must, for all practical purposes, be redone.

➤ Who Feels the Pain Must See the Gain

The telecommunications manufacturer suffered because they did not fully evaluate the business risk of the proposed sales configurator initiative. The problem and the solution were both identified and identified correctly. However, management again felt that having achieved this, it was a case of "job done." Due to this, no formal or structured assessment of potential business risk was undertaken which had fatal consequences for the project. As we will see later, our framework identifies the factors involved in undertaking such a business risk assessment.

➤ The ZAPped Manufacturer

The global manufacturing operation's problems with their ERP system were more complex and abstruse. Remember that their difficulty was that they could not put their finger on the problem per se, they just knew that none of the anticipated improvements had occurred. Therein also lies the answer. Nobody had been given individual responsibility for ensuring that the improvements would be achieved and no before-and-after metrics were available against which to verify actual outcomes. There arose a situation where everyone was looking at everyone else saying in effect, "I did my job, don't blame me." Strictly speaking, they were correct. The problem lay in the investment and benefits realization process.

To give just one example, nobody had thought to back-load supplier history into the system so that trend analysis could begin immediately, nor had any before supplier performance metrics (e.g., unmet deadlines, inaccurate deliveries) been taken. The purchasing director could claim that supplier management benefits could not be realized because nobody had loaded the required data.

■ INDUSTRIAL AGE THINKING FOR INFORMATION AGE PROBLEMS

Those five cases are instructive. They underline how much more difficult it is to achieve the benefits from IT in Eras III and IV compared to earlier times. Today's environment is faster moving and more complex. It requires not only internal integration, but also integration with trading partners while IT initiatives depend for their success on a wide range of stakeholders. Yet, as these case studies illustrate, executives extensively use Era I methodologies to address Era III and IV challenges. Industrial Age thinking for Information Age problems.

Why do we equate Industrial Age thinking with the early Eras? We attribute it partly to the dominant influence of the finance department on IT issues that, though now in decline, dominated earlier Eras. The natural tendency in the finance department is to apply techniques that were familiar and consistent with investment appraisal in other areas. This tendency was reinforced by the difficulty in evaluating intangible benefits and the consequent disillusion among executives. This factor was one of the most significant in slowing the move toward more advanced evaluation techniques. We now discuss the limitations of purely financially based techniques and the consequent impact on gaining value from IT.

■ THE LIMITATIONS OF FINANCIAL METRICS

While IT is a strategic resource and alignment between IT and the business is essential, most executives continue to place enormous emphasis on financial metrics. For this reason, relegating such measures to their appropriate place in the IT investment evaluation framework assumes high importance.

Financial measures by themselves are not sufficient measures of enterprise performance, or a basis for justifying IT investments. Organizations need a more holistic, balanced set of measures to reflect those drivers that contribute to superior performance and enterprise strategic goals. Unfortunately, as we saw, most organizations still use outmoded finance-based techniques when evaluating IT investments. These represent an essential component of the investment process, but are inadequate on their own and, in some instances, counterproductive.

➤ The Origins of Accounting

Accounting principles as we now know them originated as a mechanism for meeting legal and corporate reporting requirements. Yet, they are still used today (admittedly in a much tweaked and enhanced form) to support a range of executive decisions, including those relating to IT performance and investments—objectives that would have been far from the minds of the originators!

The accountancy-based methods such as payback, discounted cash flow, and internal rate of return reflect their Industrial Age origins, when benefits were measured in terms of enhanced input/output productivity—the factory paradigm. A wide range of elaborate attempts to apply these techniques to evaluating white-collar productivity have been undertaken, with very limited results. These attempts include accounting and financial data, stopwatch studies, task sampling, computer monitoring of keystrokes, and standard costing techniques. They all suffer from a fundamental misunderstanding of what constitutes white-collar productivity, which can be measured in such terms only when it directly parallels factory-style operations, for example, repetitive activities such as invoice production and pay calculations.

These tasks are now seldom undertaken manually, resources instead being directed toward providing faster and better data, decision support facilities, enhanced communication, and other benefits more appropriate to today's environment. Finance-based techniques also frequently equate efficiency with effectiveness. An example of this is a study that attempted to quantify management productivity. The study classified as "unproductive time" such activities as "time spent outside or within a building or waiting for meetings to start or a machine to become available."

This represents a classical Industrial Age, task-based approach to productivity. No attempt is made to evaluate the possible insights or inspiration a manager may derive from taking a walk outside. Informal discussions with colleagues before or after meetings can, on occasion, be more productive than the meeting itself. Another good illustration is the case of a customer complaints system that greatly reduced the number of follow-up calls. This had the effect, based on strict accounting measures, of reducing productivity, as measured by number of calls handled per operator. Effectiveness improved, but efficiency dropped.

Conventional measurements may not only be inadequate, but may be misleading when it comes to establishing what makes an operation perform more effectively. Consider the following example.

➤ Misleading Capital Values

Traditional accounting is not geared to capitalizing applications development or databases. This reflects the discipline's original purpose, which was to measure physical systems for delivering products and services. Very often, vast sums of money may be spent on building such applications and databases, yet they may not appear on a company's balance sheet since the accounting systems might treat them as expense items. When we consider that a newspaper title has been deemed acceptable for capitalization, it seems strange that valuable, long-term software resources disappear into the black hole of expense accounting.

This question is not one of semantics. Even though they may not qualify as capital for tax purposes, capitalizing these assets can have significant impact. An important consideration is that senior management, through being appraised of the scale of the investment, may be more inclined to apply appropriate investment management resources to it. Gartner experience suggests that the amount of time spent by senior management on IT issues bears no relation to the ratio of capital tied up in IT. Including applications software and databases should have the effect of making management focus more attention on IT issues. While information now meets most of the qualifications as an asset as demanded by the U.S. Financial Accounting Standards Board, traditional accounting techniques are unsuitable for determining the value of information.

➤ Unsuited to Today's Integrated IT Environment

As IT becomes increasingly integrated into all essential business processes and end user involvement continues to grow, few applications can be classed as truly stand alone. Most integrate with the infrastructure or with other applications in some way, if only to share a database or a printer via a network. As a consequence, evaluating potential investments as discrete, stand alone events, as accountancy-based methods inevitably must, is likely to provide an incomplete or even misleading result.

➤ Militate against Medium and Long-Term Planning

Accountancy-based methods have a built-in bias against long-term investments because the longer it takes for the financial returns to be made, the lower the present value. Whereas this is correct in terms of the time-value of money, it tends to present potential investments in IT infrastructure in a relatively unfavorable light. This militates against the formulation of well-structured IT strategic planning, showing potentially crucial requirements such as infrastructure and security in an unfavorable light. Even at the applications level, short-term considerations are likely to predominate and benefits often take longer to achieve than was originally estimated.

➤ Creates Spurious Sense of Reliability

Accounting-based techniques bias the evaluation toward the tangible cost elements and those benefits that lend themselves to easy measurement. Because something can be readily quantified, it will be included. If it cannot be readily quantified, it may well be excluded. This need not be a problem if it is recognized. However, the sheer volume of statistics and the precision with which they are applied can generate a spurious appearance of reliability. This can, and does, translate into an equally spurious feeling of satisfaction among those responsible for the evaluation process. Key areas of value-added business such as customer satisfaction, quality, speed to market, and competitive response will never be approved on the basis of measures that focus on the financially quantifiable.

➤ Backward Focus

These techniques are focused on the past, that is, what happened rather than what is happening or even will happen. Too often past experience is used as the basis for making forecasts. Especially in volatile times, this is likely to be a most unreliable indicator.

This somewhat brief review of conventional accounting-based appraisal methods shows them to be inflexible, geared toward assessing efficiency rather than effectiveness, incapable of incorporating intangible or amorphous benefits, and weak on integration. They will generally favor the safe, short-term investments over the longer term strategic and infrastructure investments. Yet, these latter investments may be essential for business success. They also neglect a formal assessment of risk, which, as will be seen later, can be a major consideration. These qualities remarkably parallel those that gave rise to the present poor performance of IT as detailed earlier. This is to be expected, because they reflect their origins in hierarchical, task-oriented, organizational structures, stemming from another time, which are unsuited for today's business environment. Again, Industrial Age thinking for Information Age problems.

This is not to say that such methods do not have a role. ROI, based on realistic cost benefit analysis, is, particularly when discounted, a vital component of most evaluation exercises. However, it is only one component. The problem today is that the formalized evaluation process in so many organizations continues to rely on these methods—in particular, the cost-benefit analysis (CBA)—alone. The CBA has severe limitations that need to be recognized.

➤ Limitations of the CBA Approach

The CBA approach is:

> ➤ *Crude:* Before-and-after estimates of benefit are crude in that they will be accurate only if work patterns remain unaltered after the implementation of the system.

Apart from instances where faster hardware is installed to run an existing computer-based system, this is unlikely to apply. Work patterns almost always change, usually by the elimination of the more routine tasks. But does that work if you're measuring the end product rather than the intermediate steps?

➤ *Misleading:* The introduction of a new application involves additional expense in terms of software and software maintenance and possibly hardware and other costs. Except where these can be directly assigned to a specific user department, they must be absorbed as overhead. Frequently, this overhead will not be taken into consideration in estimating the costs and benefits. Even when it is, the allocation will be the subject of a certain amount of arbitrariness. For example, if there is spare processing capacity, will the new system be allocated a proportion of processor costs? Should it? In the absence of a consistent approach to these issues, misleading interpretations may result.

➤ *Inadequate:* Such measures are inadequate for certain types of work, particularly those in the service sector that is forming an increasingly large proportion of economic output. For example, in professional services, with computerized assistance, an accountant may be able to produce more sets of accounts, or a lawyer more opinions, in a given time. This would be seen as increased productivity. Yet, depending on the amount of work on hand, this could actually result in a net reduction in charged time and therefore reduced earnings for the practice. Depending on how we view the issue, productivity gains could range from negative to enormous!

➤ *Cannot accommodate the growth of overheads:* Direct material and labor, which previously represented an overwhelming proportion of the cost of production, have now been overtaken by overhead costs. Take the example of the microchip, for which material and direct labor now comprise only 11 percent of manufacturing costs—and this percentage will decline. This trend renders the unit cost efficiency approach an increasingly less appropriate measure of business value.

➤ *Leads to incomprehensible complexity:* Paul Strassman has used the phrase "micromyopia" to represent what he saw as the tendency to break a problem down into increasingly smaller components when it could not at first be understood. This theory rests on the illusion that all office tasks can be broken down into minute, controllable elements. If this is accepted, all tasks can be evaluated individually, timed and controlled, and therefore measured in terms of productivity. This complexity undermines senior management's understanding and opens the way for manipulation by the cognoscenti. Although this danger is now receding as a better understanding of the dynamics of office productivity begins to take hold, the idea that deeper analysis leads to deeper understanding still has adherents.

■ THE VALUE OF FINANCIAL TECHNIQUES FOR IT INVESTMENT APPRAISAL

Having identified the limitations of these techniques, their valuable characteristics should not be overlooked. One of the most important of these is the time-value of money concept. This, in essence, states that the faster a given benefit is achieved, or the longer a given cost is deferred, the greater the value. This recognizes that, like any other resource, money also has a cost. Two techniques that accommodate the time-value of money are Net Present Value (NPV) and the Internal Rate of Return (IRR). These, and other financially related concepts, are reviewed in more detail in Appendix A.

■ WHAT ELSE DO WE NEED?

We've covered a lot of ground in this chapter, but hopefully the main objective has been achieved, namely, convincing you that financially based measurement, while playing a vital role in evaluating IT investment, nonetheless represents only one role in the overall process of successfully investing and extracting benefits. What are the others? Our framework recommends that you assess potential investments through five perspectives (including the financial one), or as we prefer to call them, the *Five Pillars of Benefits Realization*. First a brief summary to set them in context, then a more detailed look in Chapter 2.

1. *Strategic Alignment:* The alignment of IT investment strategy with the realization of the organization's business goals and objectives.
2. *Business Process Impact:* The impact on the requirement for the company to redesign business processes, more closely integrate the supply chain, or similar process-intensive initiatives.
3. *Architecture:* The integration, scalability, and resilience of the databases, operating systems, applications, and networks that the company has and/or plans to implement.
4. *Direct Payback:* The conventionally understood benefits a project can deliver, such as cost savings and better information.
5. *Risk:* Identifying the exposure of the proposed investment to failure or underachievement.

At first glance, all of these considerations might appear intimidating to senior executives who may be dazzled by the immense opportunities successful IT deployment offers. The good news is that there is a way to successfully invest in IT. There is a way to derive the benefits in a way that keeps open a wide range of options to accommodate changes in your business and technology environment. There is an Information Age solution that you can deploy. Ultimately, it comes down to good management processes and a best-practice methodology that is fully understood and accepted by the key stakeholders. Gartner has such a methodology based on the Five Pillars. It's one that has been successfully used in a range of organizations and has provided a source of reassurance for business and technology executives worldwide. This book shows you how to deploy this methodology in your organization and how to set up the governance processes to support it.

■ SUMMARY

We have seen from the case studies and the evolution over the four Eras that simplistic Production Age mechanisms are no longer appropriate. But we also know that they continue to be deployed extensively. Many organizations have made determined efforts to deploy appropriate techniques, often with considerable success, and Gartner has drawn from these examples to enrich the framework proposed here. This framework thus provides an approach suitable for both beginner organizations and those at a more advanced stage. The beginners will benefit from obtaining full guidance while the more advanced will gain by comparing their current practices against the comprehensive framework provided. The key starting message is: Each investment must be viewed through a broader range of perspectives than before. We discuss this in more detail in Chapter 2.

Chapter 2

The Five Pillars of Benefits Realization

Conquerors estimate before the war begins. They consider everything.
Sun Tzu on dynamic benefits realization

The defeated also estimate before the war, but they do not consider everything. Estimating completely creates victory. Estimating incompletely causes failure.
Sun Tzu, The Art of War for Executives

This value of "estimating completely" is not a new concept (Sun Tzu lived thousands of years ago, after all), but it is new for most executives charged with making investments in IT. We saw several examples of this in the previous chapter. As in Sun Tzu's time, those who do not do so experience failure. While modesty would forbid us from claiming that our framework estimates completely, this is a very practical approach in a wide number of engagements. The comprehensiveness of our approach stems from the three Ps of our framework—Pillars, Process, and People:

➤ *Pillars:* The Five Pillars of Benefits Realization (strategic alignment, business process impact, architecture, direct payback, risk) define the umbilical cord between business context and IT investment management. They provide the critical set of perspectives with which to understand, evaluate, manage, and retire your IT investments. They can be sculpted or customized to fit your specific business context and reshaped over time as your business context evolves.

➤ *Process:* Defines how you put the Five Pillars (5P) to work weighting their relative importance, defining the business-specific value standards (evaluation criteria) that comprise them, analyzing and managing IT initiatives against them, and keeping them up to date.

➤ *People:* Defines the organizational roles that must be filled to ensure that the process operates and does not become a paper-based, rubber-stamping, irrelevant activity.

This structure can also be seen in terms of WHAT, HOW, and WHO:

WHAT—The comprehensive framework of the 5Ps.

HOW—The processes we use to achieve benefits realization from the 5Ps.

WHO—The people and their roles required to execute the process.

Figure 2.1 illustrates the context in which the Pillars achieve benefits from IT investments. The lowest section represents some of the main drivers of business change today. These continually contribute to and change the Business Context (the second section) on which all IT investments must be based. Remember, the Business Context drives all IT investment decisions.

The question is: How do you represent this ever-changing business context in a form that enables effective IT investment decisions? You'll remember from the case studies in Chapter 1 that problems invariably arose when management focused on achieving its immediate and narrow objective to the exclusion of other factors. Those other factors, which we call the *Five Pillars of Benefits Realization* are depicted in the third section of Figure 2.1 and are summarized in Figure 2.2. In this chapter, we

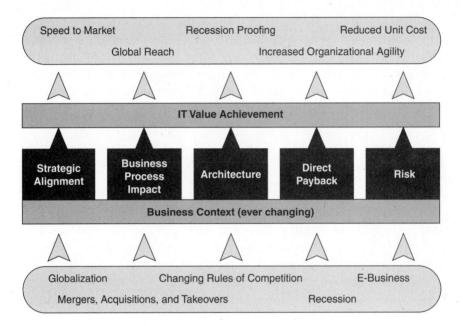

Figure 2.1 The Pillars

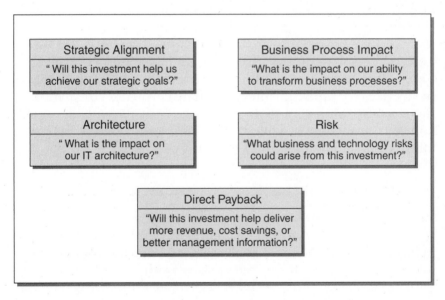

Figure 2.2 The Five Pillars of Benefits Realization

examine each one in detail and show how they contribute to the top section—IT Benefits Realization. These five Pillars will enable participants to see the whole picture when undertaking an appraisal, provide a far greater understanding of the key issues, and inform our judgment of them. For these reasons, we need to review them in some detail.

■ PILLAR 1: STRATEGIC ALIGNMENT

The fundamental shape of business is changing. The perimeters that once bounded enterprises are breaking down, economic value is shifting from goods and services to information and knowledge, and the number of people and entities that can influence enterprise objectives has soared. Enterprises have become more diffuse and amorphous as they seek ways to manage internally the changes imposed externally. Mergers and acquisitions, consolidations, standardization, integrated applications, knowledge capture, tactically oriented growth projects, temporary workforces, and process orientations all emerge as reference points in a world of uncertainty. Enterprises accustomed to defining their own business focus and market thrusts will suddenly find external forces—customers, suppliers, competitors, and governments—imposing business demands on them. Connections with buyers, suppliers, and customers will be elastic and ephemeral, expanding, contracting, or disappearing as need arises or wanes. Businesses will be defined by the nature of their relationships, by their interfaces with the outside world, and by the degree to which they seek and involve their customers and suppliers in their business processes.

► Information Technology as a Strategic Resource

Information technology is central to all of these developments. In fact, IT is becoming so powerful and transforming a medium that it will serve as the engine of innovation and the foundation of growth for enterprises worldwide. Virtually no enterprise can extend its markets, generate its products and services, communicate with suppliers and buyers, manage its investments, or communicate with its customers and employees without IT. For chief executives, IT is now the global language of business, rising to the top of the priority lists and, probably for this reason, coming under heavy examination. Business managers will no longer make business decisions without including elements of IT; and Information System (IS) organizations will no longer make technology decisions without the explicit partnership or sponsorship of the business. Indeed, enterprises that continue to treat those issues and decisions separately (a business project versus an IT project) are rapidly falling behind.

Reflecting these developments, business executives are increasingly assuming control of IT decisions, funding, and resources. The shift in power will be reflected in a shift in spending power. We now estimate that 60 percent of enterprise IT spending is controlled by business or functional managers and 40 percent by the centralized IS organization.

This increasing involvement and focus of line management on IT oversight reflects the importance of IT to the attainment of strategic business goals. IS organization and business leadership need to integrate their roles around the transformation of core business processes to take advantage of new market and operational opportunities. Due to the pervasiveness of this change, smart governance will play an increasingly key role, de-emphasizing control and oversight in favor of providing appropriate forums for both internal and external stakeholders. We'll talk about governance in detail in Chapter 3, but for now a working definition would describe it as "processes and roles that enable the organization to accomplish its overall IT goals." These governance mechanisms must facilitate fluid communications and collaboration and provide efficient connections to the mainstream business decision-making processes of the enterprise.

➤ The Winners in Era IV

The complexity of Era IV means that the enterprises' ability to apply IT to business transformation, revenue generation, and operational excellence will separate the leaders from the followers. As we saw, business models will change as IT first enables and then drives new sources of revenue. Business and IT are inseparable, with no decision resting entirely in the domain of either business or IT. All decisions should fuse together with significant implications for projects, funding streams, business priorities, budgeting, workforce preparation, risk management, and downstream costs.

As business decisions and technology decisions intertwine, the roster of interested stakeholders lengthens beyond IS and business executives. Now functional department heads, user communities, external customers, and externally sourced workers all have insight into, and influence over, the IT components in a growing number of business decisions. IS organizations that continue to keep IT decisions separate from business decisions are headed for trouble. Why? Because, it's worth repeating again, there are no *pure* IT decisions, projects, or activities. There are only business decisions, projects, and activities with varying degrees of IT intensity.

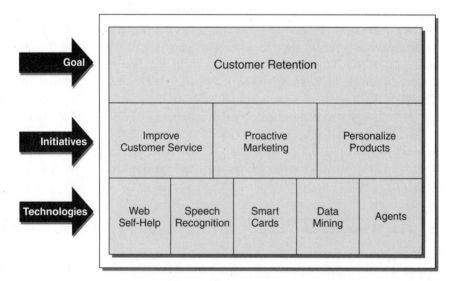

Figure 2.3   Scope: Aligning Technology and Business

It follows that the decision-making process surrounding IT investments seeks to expand IT capabilities to satisfy future business needs as well as current needs. IT investment and deployment are about assessing, allocating, and directing the use of limited resources so that IT can deliver high value in the near term and mitigate the risk of future decisions in the long term. IT is a strategic resource; consequently, investment decisions have to take into account the *strategic perspective* if they are to be effective.

With business and technology so fused, IT should become subject to the same type of measures and decisions as are other areas of the business. Executives, IS managers, and business managers will all be involved in delivering strong results, deciding or driving enterprise growth, ensuring the right technical and skill foundation for business plans, and defining which initiatives are right for the enterprise. IT will increasingly serve as underpinnings or even as drivers.

Figure 2.3 illustrates how specific initiatives can support a strategic business goal while a range of technologies in turn enables those initiatives.

Even enterprises that lack a formal strategic plan usually have a mission, set of goals, or statement of core competencies that act as a focus for investment of resources. Technologies that support these goals and initiatives are more likely to make an impact on the enterprise if they complement process and business model enhancements and are more likely to be supported by business unit and senior management.

■ PILLAR 2: BUSINESS PROCESS IMPACT

I have already referred frequently to the changes that have occurred to business models in recent years. This book is mainly about meeting the new challenges posed by these developments when it comes to investment in IT. One of the foundations of the new business paradigm is the *business process*. We'll look more at business processes shortly, but it's worthwhile to skip quickly through a little history.

Some business processes are hundreds of years old. The work principles on which we have all been brought up were based on the division of labor theory. This states that production should be broken down into a series of specialized tasks, rather than have a single person undertaking all the tasks. This goes back 200 years to Adam Smith, who showed that a number of workers performing specialized tasks could produce a far greater number of hat pins than generalists undertaking all tasks. The reduced need for training and the speed in getting workers productive were added bonuses.

The downside was that a hierarchical, or "command-and-control" management structure, with layers upon layers of supervision, was required to manage and coordinate the workers. As competition increased, the overhead costs of the command-and-control paradigm become increasingly unsustainable. Advances in technology reduced product development and deployment life cycles. Flexibility and adaptability became key requirements for which the command-and-control paradigm was distinctly unsuited. With everyone focused on their own task and their own department's role in the chain, nobody had a clear view on the effectiveness of the whole process or the impact on the customer. Success factors (following the rule book) became increasingly out of line with modern business requirements—activity rather than results. Over time, the attitude of "this is the way we've always done it" leads to accumulating inefficiencies. Computers have been effective in automating routine clerical functions (e.g., payroll, inventory control), but much less so when automating more complex business processes. These processes need to be redesigned to gain full value from IT's capabilities.

These developments lead to focusing on business activities as a series of processes rather than hierarchically controlled tasks. One way of describing a business process is as "a series of activities that combine to generate a product or service of value to the customer." (*Note:* The customer can be internal to the organization.) A process view and the resulting organizational structures are quite different from the traditional one. One of the main characteristics is to view business activities on a cross-departmental basis as distinct from a silo basis. There were also significant changes in organizational and human resource management, as illustrated in Figure 2.4.

When activities are studied for efficiency and effectiveness from a process perspective, it is often found that most were neither efficient nor effective. Typical problems included:

➤ Too much checking and reconciling.

➤ Too much work being done sequentially.

➤ A high proportion of rework, errors, credit notes, and so on.

➤ A high proportion of exceptional cases.

➤ A focus on activity rather than results.

➤ Extensive rekeying of data between systems or into spreadsheets.

➤ Bad use of assets as indicated by high levels of production or sales inventories.

➤ Unnecessary complexity.

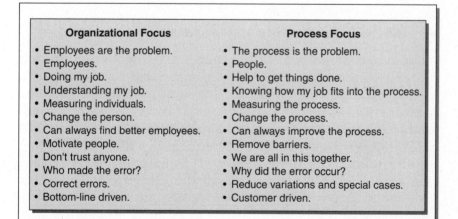

Organizational Focus	Process Focus
• Employees are the problem.	• The process is the problem.
• Employees.	• People.
• Doing my job.	• Help to get things done.
• Understanding my job.	• Knowing how my job fits into the process.
• Measuring individuals.	• Measuring the process.
• Change the person.	• Change the process.
• Can always find better employees.	• Can always improve the process.
• Motivate people.	• Remove barriers.
• Don't trust anyone.	• We are all in this together.
• Who made the error?	• Why did the error occur?
• Correct errors.	• Reduce variations and special cases.
• Bottom-line driven.	• Customer driven.

Figure 2.4 Changes in Human Resource Management

These problems naturally lead to attempts to redesign these processes, taking various forms such as process improvement, process redesign, process reengineering, and so on. Much hype surrounded such methodologies and overblown claims were made. However, there is no doubt that new business models drove the need to radically transform business processes. Important determinants for such transformation include:

➤ All options are kept open—the process is viewed as a green field site.

➤ The customer (internal or external) is the key focus for all improvement efforts.

➤ Power is devolved as far as possible to the people doing the job.

➤ Combine several jobs into one whenever possible.

➤ Departmental boundaries are of less importance— achieving the goals of the process is the primary consideration.

➤ Process redesign initiatives rely on information technology to some degree.

➤ Task elements of the process are performed simultaneously rather than sequentially.

➤ The Onset of Trading Partner Processes

While much progress has been made in rationalizing internal processes, the explosive growth of e-business is, as we have seen earlier, leading to much closer integration between business partners (and even competitors on occasion). In fact, Gartner forecasts that 70 percent of new application investment and 50 percent of new infrastructure investment by 2005 will be driven by e-business. This combination of evolving business drivers, changing customer demands, and the evolution of enabling technology, is producing a business revolution that relegates enterprise-focused IT applications to niche component status. E-business and electronic connections are changing the way enterprises deal with partners, information access, services, and speed as key differentiators. Web connections enable collaboration between enterprises, making it critical to optimize business processes across enterprises rather than just within an enterprise.

Future success depends on integrated business processes (IBPs) realigned to provide value in terms of packaging customized services and products for each individual client. Enterprises are, thus, morphing from vertically integrated supply chains to interconnected ecosystems of suppliers and customers. This means that today most businesses are linked by processes that run upstream to suppliers and downstream to intermediaries and customers. The trend is to focus on core capabilities and link up with other companies to provide the rest, increasing the number of connections. There are also many services available over the Web that companies are now building into their processes. To optimize potential, enterprises are using IBPs to create new business models, gain access to new markets, create value from what companies do individually and what they do jointly. IBPs also enable enterprises to proceed in a sense-and-respond way. This collaboration forms a common business process between partners. Value is added by what partners do individually and jointly.

Figure 2.5 defines the key components of integrated processes in an e-business environment. The focus is away from hierarchies and reporting structures to flexible relationships and roles. The result is very different from what we have all become used to.

The IBP design is likely to require existing IT systems to be modified in some way, new systems to be created, and/or architecture to be modified. If this is not done in a coordinated way, there is a danger that IS cohesiveness may be lost. Managing these changes, and the consequent IT investments, requires strong IS governance mechanisms—at a minimum, it requires a dedicated team responsible for designing and policing the architecture. The architecture needs to be flexible to support the IBP and allow it to change, and at the same time protect other IT assets, such as legacy systems.

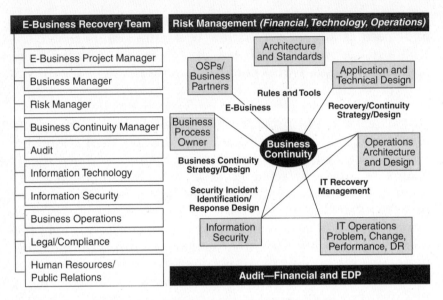

Figure 2.5 E-Business—Integrated Processes

We can make a number of conclusions about business processes, including:

➤ They are assuming critical importance in all enterprise operations.

➤ Business processes, especially those that span trading partners, are enabled by IT and crucially dependent on it.

➤ Any proposed IT investment that fails to take this perspective into account risks failure.

Consider the following:

Processes Today Are Highly Dependent on Disparate Applications

Processes generally transcend a number of departmental applications, even applications belonging to trading partners. For the process to operate effectively, it needs to consolidate and rationalize data from those applications, synchronize updates, and generally have one version of the truth. In such circumstances, replacing a component application would have significant impact on process effectiveness.

Latest Enterprise Software Is Often Architected around Processes

Many modern applications, such as ERP systems, are process based. That is, rather than the stovepipe, departmentally based applications of earlier eras, they are architected around processes (e.g., the stock replenishment process). These are based on best practice as applied to specific situations, and the so-called "vanilla" versions can be implemented without customization. This greatly reduces implementation time and increases reliability, with the trade-off being the need for the client company to change its work practices in line with those of the application.

The implication of this for new IT investment is that such processes are now inextricably bound into the software. So, for example, if you have an ERP system in place and want to introduce CRM, you could face a lot of trouble because the processes required to support CRM might not interact effectively with those of the ERP system. And there would be considerable interaction between them. Think again about the ZAPped Manufacturer case study. This company's production scheduling system needed to interface with the planned ERP application. Prior to the introduction of the ERP system, the company implemented integration software designed to ensure consistency of data, that is, iron out all semantic and syntax problems between the two applications. However, when the ERP was implemented, it was found that the business processes embodied in its software were incompatible with those related to the production scheduling system. One of the problems was that the ERP process needed the data in real time while the other process collected in batch mode once a day, based on the work practices in the plant. This meant that the ERP's forward planning and stock replenishment modules were acting on inaccurate data. The result was not catastrophic, but it did cause problems and inaccuracies,

> ## PILLAR 2: BUSINESS PROCESS IMPACT
>
> In short, business processes and IT are two sides of the same coin. Change one and you affect the other. In fact, it goes beyond individual applications, in that the underlying electronic messaging systems such as e-mail, but more particularly workflow and groupware, have a large and growing role in the effective operation of business processes. It is therefore crucial to take business process impact into account when investing in IT.

which required a multitude of spreadsheets to resolve—never a good idea. Eventually the work practices had to be changed but at considerable cost and disruption to the enterprise.

Strategic Implications of Software-Embedded Processes

Embedding processes in software can also have strategic implications. For instance, an enterprise might operate under conditions whereby a merger or acquisition and/or closer trading links with partners are being considered. Or an enterprise might operate in a highly dynamic, volatile, and unpredictable environment, like so many new e-business ventures today. In such circumstances, embedding business processes in software would negatively impact the capacity to integrate systems with new business partners, and would undermine the flexibility to respond to changed business circumstances. Many organizations have already discovered this to their disadvantage.

■ PILLAR 3: ARCHITECTURE

Within Pillar 2, I referred to the extent to which businesses closely interact with trading partners, with this interaction heavily dependent on IT. Under the broad classification of e-business, organizations across the globe now collaborate in real time. The impetus of e-business and virtually integrated enterprise (VIE) is extending the reach and range of business relationships. Meanwhile, IT and telecommunications have converged to enable work practices that were previously considered nonviable. By changing how, when, where, and with whom people communicate and collaborate, these forces are having a substantial impact on the IT architecture. Its role and complexity are growing to enable and sustain the *anywhere, any time* speed-based, agile environment that characterizes e-business work styles. The key dynamics are *flexibility* and *choice*. The trick is to accomplish it without losing the benefits of standardization.

In this section, we'll look at some of the many ways that architecture can impact the achievement of IT value and some architectural best practice principles.

➤ The Impact of E-Business on Architecture

Typical e-business objectives include:

- ➤ Creating a single profile for each and every client to facilitate mass customization, enhanced customer service, and inimitable product/service development.
- ➤ Virtually integrating suppliers, strategic partners, and clients to focus on core competencies and improved agility.
- ➤ Turning corporate information into leveragable insights.

Other imperatives include:

- ➤ The capability to extend IT-enabled business processes across geographical, organizational, and technical boundaries.
- ➤ Process integration to reduce cycle times (which is predicated on the capability to rapidly integrate divergent business software applications).
- ➤ Knowledge management, which cannot fuel innovation without a consolidated, consistent view of corporate data.

➤ Support for knowledge workers, who cannot work from home or on the road unless their supporting technologies are portable and reliable any time, anywhere.

➤ The capacity to quickly and closely integrate the business operations and processes of other companies where a takeover or merger is involved.

➤ What We Mean by the Term IT Architecture

These objectives inherently depend on an enabling IT architecture. The term *IT architecture* may be somewhat ambiguous. For our purposes, we specify it as the approved hardware platforms, operating systems, database management systems (DBMSs), development tools, middleware services, or other

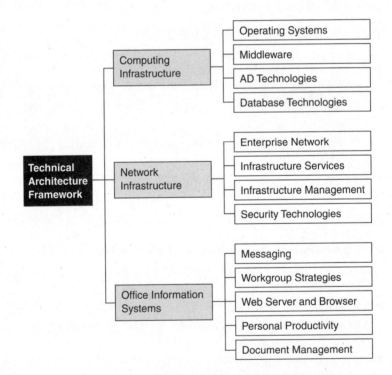

Figure 2.6 Technical Architecture Framework

products. As Figure 2.6 shows, Gartner divides the technical architecture into three main subgroups: Computing Infrastructure, Network Infrastructure, and Office Information Systems. These are subdivided into elements as shown.

Often the IT architecture is specified in terms of formal standards (e.g., ANSI SQL, Posix 1003.1, XPG) to reduce vendor lock-in. For the purposes of this exercise, I am extending the term to include what we normally refer to as the "information" or "application" architecture in the overall architecture term. This is the specification of the functions and interfaces of the component parts of a system or a set of systems. The Gartner Technology Architecture Framework (Figure 2.6) shows the components of an enterprise's architecture, while Figure 2.7

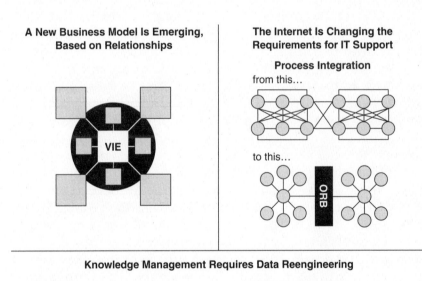

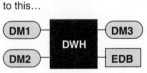

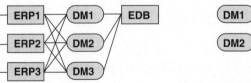

Figure 2.7 "Clicks"—The Technological Infrastructure

illustrates the architectural impact of technological developments in terms of new business models, IT support, and data reengineering.

The middleware referred to in Figure 2.6 may include basic communication facilities, such as, message-oriented middleware (MOM), file transfer services, screen scrapers, database gateways; an integration broker or two; business process managers; business activity monitors; message warehouse; development; administrative; Metadata (message dictionary); security services; and optional gateways and adapters for independent software vendor (ISV) packages. Enterprises that fail to standardize their integration middleware will end up with expensive and complex nervous systems, too many MOM products, too many integration brokers, too many business process managers, too many point solutions, and other redundancies. The full awfulness of this is illustrated in Figure 2.8 and underlines what can result from bad architectural planning.

If you are from the business side of your organization, you don't have to understand the technicalities of these and other architecture-related issues. The governance structures recommended later on will insulate you from this. The key point is to know enough to appreciate the potential significance of these factors when you are considering an investment.

Architecture from an information perspective should provide central design guidance to enable the development of high-quality, mutually compatible application systems. If you build applications using common data, object, and process models, you'll generally find it easier to exchange objects, files, messages, and documents. Business processes that span multiple systems can more easily be implemented. With proper planning, components can be reused via source code copying, object-oriented inheritance, or service-oriented architecture invocations.

Successful enterprises today design flexibility into their architectures to facilitate rapid change. There are many benefits to an open-systems-based IT infrastructure that uses standardized, reusable components and leverages Internet, wireless, and middleware technologies. It can best support

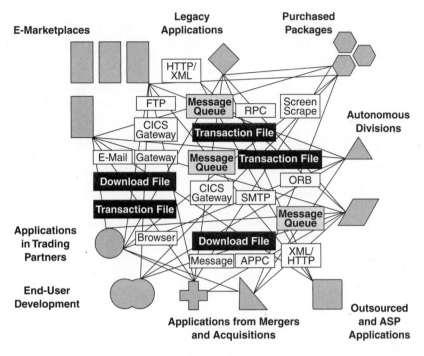

Figure 2.8 Integration Spaghetti

current business-application requirements and rapid change while being both scalable and extensible. However, as Figure 2.9 shows, there are many impediments to implementing such an architecture. Many organizations face challenges in all of the areas referred to, so don't expect to overcome them entirely. As you work through our methodology, you'll see how it helps you balance the need for good architecture against other competing requirements.

The explosion of personal devices is one such challenge. Options for personal devices are becoming more varied, from PCs to palmtops, to network computers, to Webtops, to cellular phones; many functions are being cross-adopted in a convergence of functionality across alternatives. Due to the increasing diversity of contact choices available to customers, successful applications will be designed with multiple delivery mechanisms in mind. This will be represented by a combination of

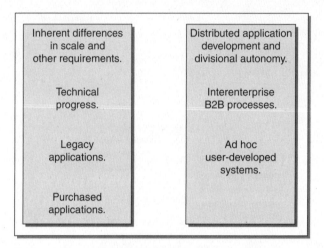

Figure 2.9 Impediments to Technical Uniformity

cell phone, Internet, fax, snail mail, and human contact that must be seamlessly integrated to meet customers' needs in the future.

Many enterprises today have constructed parallel islands, offering similar services to customers who choose Web, voice response, in-store, telephone, and fax access. Unfortunately, these islands do not work together, locking the customer into the island of first contact at a time when he or she might wish to transition to a more convenient electronic world (e-world) or physical world (p-world) contact.

Business processes and business tools must reach both the e-world and the p-world in a consistent and coherent manner to match the movements of customers in and out of those worlds as the customers choose. Customers, after all, choose how they want to interact with the vendor.

➤ The Legacy Challenge

A key impediment not referred to in this diagram, but one faced by most organizations, is the existing systems that continue to function and provide value to an organization. Sometimes called legacy systems, these applications still provide a huge proportion of IT capability, despite the mass replacements arising from Y2K. These applications often embody enterprise-specific functionality not easily replicated by newer off-the-shelf products. However, they usually lack the flexibility and openness needed for today's environment. As we saw in the manufacturing case study in Chapter 1, modern applications will often rely on legacy transaction processing systems for their core transaction data. Thus, the capacity of such applications to integrate with legacy systems becomes a very important consideration in an investment decision.

Legacy extension can, in many instances, provide a practical solution to quickly solve the problem without invasive modifications. Many legacy extension solutions can reduce the risk of modification or transformation in a noninvasive way, which is frequently impossible with new object, component, or messaging solutions. Flexibility can be enabled and application integration provided while reducing the risk of failure or diminished capability. This approach represents a viable first step, but should be seen as just that, a first step. Organizations should plan for more robust application integration solutions as the new needs of e-business merge with the old application values of reliability, availability, and serviceability.

The challenges in integrating old and new technologies should not be underestimated. Readers with a technical interest will know that differences in the calling/parameter structure between COBOL, BAL, PL/1, Java, and C++ need resolution. The isolation of processing and data, a requirement of components/objects, is contrary to the common working storage and coding structures of most legacy programs, which would be structured as procedural. Differences in data types must also be resolved. Parameters passed between programs of differing languages or platforms introduce additional layers of complexity. Most importantly, changing procedural programs (from interprogram process flow to cross-module, cross-platform flow) requires restructuring of the interface logic. It also involves middleware connectivity decisions and run time environments.

When executives assess a potential new IT investment, therefore, they will need to consider the impact on, and of, legacy applications. Decisions will need to be made on the extent to which these applications can be (or need to be) upgraded or extended, their likely lifespan, availability of systems and programming documentation, performance, and synchronization (many if not most such applications operate in batch mode) and skill sets required. It may well be that, having undertaken such an evaluation, the original scope of the investment will need to be changed, perhaps substantially. I have consulted with an enterprise that implemented a new ERP system on the assumption that it would integrate adequately with the existing work scheduling application. It did so technically, but the changed business processes demanded by the ERP resulted in the scheduling application being virtually unworkable, which gave rise to immense problems in manufacturing.

An architecture is intended to achieve one or more of the following four goals:

1. Maximize application portability or interoperability through hardware and software consistency.

2. Reduce the number of redundant products in use, so that the technical staff does not have to maintain knowledge of many products (e.g., decrease staffing/training costs).

3. Save effort in the procurement process because, after the initial product selection, subsequent purchases will not require reinvestigating the competing alternatives.

4. Achieve revenue savings by buying large quantities from a single vendor (e.g., buying an enterprise license).

In conclusion, to achieve maximum business value, the architecture should:

➤ Be flexible enough to accommodate the rapidly changing demands of today's business environment, yet sufficiently robust to support mission-critical applications.

➤ Provide the basis for competitive advantage through the application of technology, yet include the capacity to respond rapidly in the event of a threat of competitive

---

Pillar 3: Architecture

The IT architecture is vital in navigating through today's constantly changing, speed-based business environment. It is the connective tissue between business strategy, processes, organization, and technology, explicitly defining the role of infrastructure in realizing business strategy. It establishes the guiding principles that will be used in selecting, implementing, integrating, and managing shared resources, and ultimately drives the business's portfolio of supported infrastructure methodologies and technologies. One of the main reasons that enterprises fail to realize the business value expected, is that they underestimate the complexities of extending processes across divergent technology platforms, and they lack a comprehensive plan for integration or consolidation. A comprehensive assessment of the architectural impact is recommended as part of the investment process.

---

technological lockout. In other words, to be able not only to apply competitive lockout but also to respond to lockout initiatives by competitors.

➤ Maximize the economic benefits and independence stemming from utilizing a range of vendors, yet avoid the risks of incompatibility and vendor financial instability.

➤ Provide adequate security and data access controls while minimizing user inconvenience.

➤ Provide maximum practical protection for existing investments yet be in a position to exploit new technologies as they come to fruition.

■ PILLAR 4: DIRECT PAYBACK

Finance-based techniques such as CBA will not provide an adequate basis for investment decisions. Strategic alignment, architecture, business process impact, and a structured risk assessment are essential. However, we must never forget the consideration that is closest to the hearts of all executives: What benefits will the investment bring? Or, what is the return on investment or direct payback?

This perspective examines the nature of the elements that are seen to contribute toward direct payback and categorizes the elements of value added. Given the trend away from so-called hard benefits toward those of the more intangible variety, we need to establish firmer criteria for evaluating the latter.

➤ Financial Return

Virtually every project requires a satisfactory financial return, whether that verdict is rendered with analytic integrity or deductively derived. Regardless of the means by which it is derived, project champions (a powerful advocate of the project) are responsible for delivering the outcome. Preparing a financial analysis to underpin a project is the stage fraught with the most bureaucracy, hypocrisy, and dogma. Executive management does not approve a project without an acceptable financial return, the basis of which is specific to each enterprise.

Many breakthrough projects require significant changes in operating methods and accurate forecasting of the financial impact is virtually impossible. As a result, it is common for financial assumptions to be deductively derived to justify a project that is deemed necessary. For example, the forecast revenue and margin for a hypothetical e-commerce project that conveniently produces a required 16 percent return has different flavors of financial impact such as increased revenue, reduced costs, and cost avoidance.

A much more favorable financial impact is required from cost avoidance projects, because their value to the enterprise is viewed as more tentative. Moreover, projects that reduce indirect labor are viewed skeptically, because it is often impossible to measure any tangible impact. Unfortunately for IS organizations, this last category is where many projects fail.

For instance, everyone is confident that a well-managed help desk can reduce expenses and improve enterprise productivity. However, proving those beliefs requires tremendous discipline and thoroughness. It is unlikely that staffing levels outside the support staff are measurably reduced, even if people are more efficiently supported. Because of the frequent inability to demonstrate the tangible impact of an IT project, project champions are often vigorously challenged and many worthwhile projects go unfunded.

The essential concept of capital budgeting within a typical enterprise is that capital is allocated using an annualized rationing process. Typical enterprises establish an enterprise wide budget and then select capital projects based on their short, medium, and long-term impacts on the financial statements and their contribution and relevance to enterprise strategy. This process means that the likelihood of any single project being funded is a function of the project itself, as well as the other capital projects that happen to be competing with it. One of the implications of this for project champions is that capital rationing establishes a competitive forum for project funding. As a result, successful project champions are aware of other major projects being considered in the same time frame as the project they are proposing.

Many different ways exist to measure financial payback, and techniques vary widely. Many individuals and enterprises have strong positions regarding the relative merits of one financial measurement tool compared to another. In Gartner's view, each measure provides insight from one perspective, but does not provide a complete picture. We recommend that project champions clearly understand the unique house style that their enterprise requires, and ensure that their project proposals include that analysis.

➤ Benefits Classification

In any discussion of IT benefits there seem to be as many definitions as there are participants. There are two types of benefits: tangible and intangible. A tangible benefit can be defined as one that directly impacts an enterprise's bottom line, such as a direct cost savings or revenue generation. The intangible variety is one that brings about improvement in business performance, but not in a way that directly impacts the bottom line. An example of this would be one that improves management information or the security of the firm.

➤ Tangible Benefits

As we saw in the brief history review in Chapter 1, in the early days of computing, investments were made almost exclusively on the basis of tangible benefits and these generally related to cost savings of some form or other. The opportunities for such savings have now been greatly reduced. Nonetheless, opportunities do exist and senior management continues to look to this area for justification of IT investments. Accordingly, it still merits attention in the appraisal process.

We next discuss the more common forms of direct benefits.

➤ Cost Savings

Cost savings apply where the proposed system reduces or eliminates costs to a degree exceeding the investment and operational costs. This is the most simple and direct form of tangible benefit, although sometimes complicated by the issue of cost avoidance as against cost displacement.

Staff Displacement

The most common form of cost saving traditionally related to staff displacement—in the 1980s "headcount reduction" was almost like a mantra. In an IT investment context, staff displacement normally occurs when routine clerical or administrative tasks, such as order processing or inventory control, are computerized, with related staff losing their jobs or being reassigned. Sometimes the savings may relate to overtime and/or travel avoidance. Savings can also occur without staff displacement or reassignment when a system allows increased volumes, or greater complexity, to be handled by the same number of staff.

Quality Control

Systems that facilitate improved quality control can and should give rise to direct cost savings. These can take tangible form by way of reduced reworking, fewer rejections at final inspection, fewer customer returns, and reduced help-desk requirements.

Reduced Computer Costs

The general improvement in the price/performance ratio of computers usually means reduced capital and maintenance costs for new equipment. In addition, software maintenance costs generally increase in line with the age of the system.

Other Cost Savings

IT provides almost unlimited scope to make savings throughout the value chain. Inventory control systems can lead to savings on cash flow, floor space, and employee time. Similar savings can be made by way of production control systems while financial control systems can generate savings on cash flow and reduce misapplication of company resources.

➤ Revenue Creation

New Product Introduction

Some systems (particularly in the financial services) enable totally new products to be introduced or provide economic justification for hitherto unacceptable products.

Increased Sales Revenue

The promise of increased sales appears to be a common justification for IT investments. Whereas such benefits would normally

---

PILLAR 4: DIRECT PAYBACK

Direct Payback is what many people consider the real reason for investing in IT, and hence hardly needs justification. The ultimate objective of almost all IT investment is to deliver business value as represented by the elements covered by this Pillar. But—crucially—to achieve Direct Payback, your investments must also succeed across the other Pillars.

---

be classified as intangible, the promise can be categorized as tangible when, for example, the unit cost of a product can be reduced, providing additional net revenue for an unchanged level of sales.

■ PILLAR 5: RISK

The forces which have given rise to the need for a new paradigm in IT investment appraisal have had a similar impact on risk assessment. The increased importance of organizational and human resource considerations, a turbulent business environment, rapid and unpredictable change, and the emergence of quality and service as key performance criteria have added a new dimension of complexity in assessing risk. The pervasiveness of IT in organizational structures, giving rise to a move from financial criteria toward those of a more subjective and qualitative nature, has created a similar requirement in the area of risk assessment. This assumption is borne out by the high proportion of failed projects and benefits leakage from many successful ones.

In light of this, you might assume that risk would be at or near the top of the agenda when executives plan to invest in IT. However, the reverse is true. Most organizations will consider the risks, but in an unstructured and inconsistent way. Few undertake a structured, comprehensive, and methodical approach to investment risk and risk management. The resulting disappointment should not come as a surprise.

Getting projects approved often is a matter of personal credibility, generally the project champion's and the sponsor's. From this perspective, having a project successfully challenged by a functional risk manager questioning financial, environmental, legislative, or safety issues is the surest way to have one's personal credibility undermined and is something to be avoided at all costs. The only way to overcome these hurdles is to thoroughly understand the risks and address them as part of the project plan. It is very much a case of going slow up-front to build consensus and then going fast at the end because the hurdles have been mapped. It is a lot of work, but in most enterprises this is the most effective path to securing project approval. We now discuss some common areas of risk.

➤ Organizational Risks

Strength of Alignment with Business Objectives

The risk of the project not aligning with business objectives is potentially one of the most serious, and has grown in importance in line with that of strategic alignment. The rate of business and technological change that characterizes today's business environment makes this consideration at once both more important and more difficult. A further complication arises from the capacity of an IT investment to act as a catalyst for business change, and conversely, to act as an impediment if it turns out to embed outdated practices in software or hardware. Factors adding to the risk would be imprecise or contradictory objectives, a turbulent external environment resulting in the need for frequent revisions of objectives, or inadequate processes for linking business and IT strategies. (This factor could also be considered under the Strategic Alignment perspective.)

Culture

The risk cultures of organizations vary considerably. For example, the attitude to risk taking in a government department, to take one extreme, is likely to be considerably different from that in a high technology company seeking to enter or even create new markets. The government department, or a similar type organization, is more likely to set a high premium on a careful, well-documented approach to risk, using well-known and reliable suppliers, applying a minimum of innovation. Such an organization would set a high premium on following prescribed guidelines and procedures, against which any subsequent failures or shortcomings in the project would be evaluated. By way of contrast, the organization on the opposite end of the spectrum would see risk taking as an essential element of competitive advantage. This may result in purchasing relatively untried hardware or software, perhaps from financially unstable suppliers, or specifying ambitious implementation deadlines. The organizational culture is such that risks such as these are deemed to be acceptable.

Organizational Preparedness

The organizational impact of many systems can be considerable. A new IT initiative can cause changes in job definition, power structures, career prospects, the degree of job security, departmental influence, or ownership of data. Any one or combination of these factors could have an impact on the success of the project, and with IT becoming increasingly embedded in core business processes, such considerations assume greater importance. Gartner research shows that organizations vary widely in the extent of their preparedness for such outcomes. For example, a long-established, hierarchical, task-oriented organization may find it much more difficult to adapt compared to an organization that is modern and flexible, with a flat organizational structure.

Management Support

The degree of management support for an investment in IT is crucial, and assumes added significance as IT plays an increasingly important role in organizational redesign.

➤ Project Risks

Project Management Skills

Project management skills are crucial for a successful implementation, yet are often overlooked or confused with general development staff capabilities. I witnessed a project where the staff were all high caliber and well motivated. Yet, the project ran both behind time and over budget due to a fall-down in project management. The assumption was that with staff of such a caliber, strong project management skills were not required. That's not the case in my experience.

Size and Duration

It has been repeatedly demonstrated that the exposure to risk varies markedly with the size and duration of the project. The bigger the project and the longer it takes to complete, the bigger the risk. Research has shown the laws of complexity apply to the number of components or individuals associated in a project. That is, the difficulties and problems increase exponentially with the number of factors.

An accurate estimation of size and duration calls for a realistic appreciation of development staff output. This is often postulated on the best case principle at the planning stage, that is, each member of the development team has his or her contribution determined on the basis of what he or she is capable of producing in a given day. What is capable of being produced and what actually is produced can vary widely however. Studies have shown that such productivity is, in fact, about half what it should have been in theory, with factors such as machine downtime, meetings, paperwork, other company business, sickness, personal time, and other factors, accounting for the balance.

Complexity

As with size and duration, the risk varies closely with the level of complexity, which is compounded by the number of business functions that need the new system and the number of other systems with which it must interfaced.

Functional Uncertainty

As the objective of applications moves from cost saving and automation of existing tasks to the broader meeting of corporate objectives, the risk of functional or definitional uncertainty inevitably increases. This could be reflected in the imprecise or incomplete definition of the business problem and/or the proposed business solution. This may stem from an inability of the system users to define requirements accurately or an inability of the analysts to accurately assess those requirements. The operating system, programming language(s), and development tools all have a bearing on technical uncertainty. The level of risk is closely related to the level of maturity of these components.

Hardware and Vendor Related Risk

As organizational and business issues assume increased importance, hardware dependence has shown a commensurate decline. Risks associated with the hardware component of an investment focus on meeting the delivery date, performance, and reliability. If you have reached the stage of short-listing potential, you'll need to assess the potential risk deriving from the financial strength of supplier, potential redirection of supplier strategy during the life of the project, the newness of the technology, and so on.

Capacity for Testing

The degree of testing capable of being applied for a new application will have a major impact on its eventual success, but this capability can vary significantly. The main determinants are time constraints and the extent to which existing functions are being directly replaced by the new system. The introduction of an invoicing/debtors system would represent an example of this. In this instance, it is likely that test output can be compared to predetermined values, possibly even in the context of a parallel run, that is, the new and old systems run in parallel, allowing for comprehensive, real-life testing. As we move toward the VIE and collaborative commerce, the ability to test becomes severely curtailed. An additional risk is posed by systems that cannot be totally tested and must discount any project that cannot be fully load and process tested.

Business Continuity Planning

In the mid- to late-1990s, as technology became integral to the business processes themselves, enterprises began to realize that traditional disaster recovery plans with 72-hour recovery periods were not good enough. In fact, for many, a 72-hour outage of critical business processes would seriously damage the enterprise and potentially affect its economic viability. As a result, enterprises instituted shorter recovery time and point objectives, often between four and 24 hours. The evolution toward e-business has resulted in yet another problem affecting business continuity planning (BCP) requirements. First, for many e-businesses, a four- to 24-hour site outage would cause irreparable damage to the enterprise. Consequently, enterprises need to incorporate business continuity planning into their application and technology architecture designs, and build in continuous 24/7 availability. Second, the risks are greater with e-business so the business continuity (BC) plan must address new scenarios and BC processes must integrate with a greater number of enterprise processes, including e-fulfillment, security, performance, and problem management.

New Technology

New technology is a constant in today's environment and it always introduces heightened levels of risk. This can derive from the tendency of time pressures resulting in experimentation passing into full-fledged implementation before the completion of an adequate testing phase, leading to suboptimal results. New technology will, in addition, not be as well tested or as robust as the older variety.

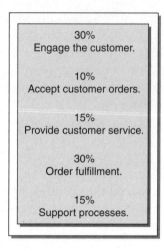

30%
Engage the customer.

10%
Accept customer orders.

15%
Provide customer service.

30%
Order fulfillment.

15%
Support processes.

Figure 2.10 Technology Is Rarely the Main Cause for Failure

E-Business Related

With 70 percent of new application investment and 50 percent of new infrastructure investment by 2005 (0.7 probability), e-business is rapidly transforming business processes. The result of the new risks and the integration of continuous availability into the business process impacts the business in new ways. The boundaries between business as usual and an emergency event that were so easily erected prior to e-commerce are no longer possible. There is no distinction between these two operating environments. As Figure 2.10 shows, technology is a relatively minor cause of failure in an e-business environment.

➤ Staff Risks

User Commitment

The level of user commitment is a key element in determining the success, and hence the level of risk, of most projects. Everyone knows of examples of applications that failed due to user opposition or lack of support. This risk can be influenced by factors such as the general quality of industrial relations, job security, standards of IT training, user-friendliness of the new system, and the degree of user involvement in design or selection.

User Capabilities

Increasingly, the success of applications depends on the capabilities of users to exploit them. This is a direct consequence of the rush toward distributed and collaborative computing, which in turn derives from characteristics of today's business environment that I have already referred to on a number of occasions. Even with the support of the users, inadequate training, experience, or implementation of an application too complex for the caliber of the user will increase the risk of failure.

Staff Stability

A high turnover of staff, particularly development staff, increases the level of risk in a project. This posed a severe problem in the late 1990s until the tech burnout of 2001, but has now somewhat declined. Nonetheless, the staff most likely to be lured away is likely to be the best, thus posing the greatest risk to the project. The capacity to recruit new staff should be a factor in the risk assessment, but induction time into a development team can be an important consideration.

➤ External Environment

Competitive Action

This is likely to represent a very significant external risk for most organizations. Action taken by a competitor may have direct impact on an IT project. For instance, an insurance company may be planning to introduce a claims processing system that will provide greater internal efficiencies and information. This project could be jeopardized by a competitor introducing a system that provides enhanced service levels to the customer. This competitive development could result in the project being abandoned and replaced by one incorporating matching levels of service.

Government Legislation

New legislation, or changes to existing legislation, can impact the risk profile of a project. The potential impact varies according to the industry. A good example relates to the deregulation of the aircraft industry. It had far-reaching ramifications for every airline and affected IT by way of generating requirements for new applications, changes to existing ones, and greater emphasis on cost control and payback. Government initiatives can have even more impact in the public sector. The growth of e-business has given rise to a tremendous amount of new legislation and it is still very far from complete. Some of this could have major systems impact.

The Economy

Economic performance can impact the financial well-being of a company in a variety of ways, and therefore its capacity to allocate project resources. The economy can also influence the competitive environment, either favorably or unfavorably, with possible impact on project requirements or resources.

PILLAR 5: RISK

In reality, given the extent of IT project failure and disappointment, it is hardly necessary to emphasize the need to include risk as a perspective. The many factors just covered underline this, and in fact the number of potential risk elements is infinitely greater, which vary between organizations, and indeed within organizations, over time. The key to successful investing and subsequent risk management is to undertake a *structured* approach. Like so many other elements associated with investment appraisal and benefits realization, most enterprises address the issue, but in an unbalanced and incomplete way, often focusing on that which is obvious, or easily measured. Our recommendation is that a formal, structured risk analysis is an essential perspective for evaluating IT investments.

Revisiting the Case Studies in Light of the Five Pillars

The term "pillar" is justified when we see the extent to which these perspectives could have helped in the five case studies detailed in Chapter 1, and which we can now revisit.

The Gung-Ho CEO

This company focused almost exclusively on Direct Payback. While circumstances justified affording this Pillar the most emphasis, or to put it another way, the highest weighting, the exclusive emphasis caused the problems, and the application's premature demise. Had the Architecture Pillar been taken into account, the unsuitability of the underlying operating system and hardware, and the implications of this, would have quickly come to light. In a similar way, the Business Process Impact assessment would have shown that business processes were to be embedded in the software. This is not necessarily a bad thing, but in this case it was, given the CEO's plans.

The Secretive Bank

This is a glaring example of overlooking the Strategic Alignment Pillar. One of the most common issues to be addressed under this Pillar is that of possible mergers, takeovers, or acquisitions. The investment framework that Gartner uses, and which is the subject of this book, would ensure that top executives would have been informed of the implications of this issue and required them to address it in the light of this knowledge. In such circumstances, there would surely have been a more satisfactory outcome.

Silo Myopia

The previous bank ignored Strategic Alignment, and this bank ignored the Architecture Pillar. Driven by the need for speed and intense user pressure, point solutions were deployed in the absence of a consistent data architecture, resulting in stand-alone stovepipes of little value to the corporation. A structured review of the Business Process Impact Pillar would also have alerted the evaluation team to this and related problems.

Who Feels the Pain Must Feel the Gain

Risk was the Pillar not adequately addressed with this telecommunications equipment provider. One of our Risk standards is organizational impact, and within that we may look for situations where the users of a new application have nothing to gain from its introduction (i.e., who feels the pain must feel the gain). In this case, the users perceived it to be an actual impediment. The structured risk assessment would also have identified the half-hearted user involvement in the design as a further likely source of problems.

What about the case of the ZAPped manufacturer? The reasons for those problems relate much more to the other two Pillars, Process and People, and these will be covered in Chapters 3 and 4.

■ SUMMARY

This revisiting of the case studies underlines a set of common problems in IT, most of which would have been avoided had they been assessed using the Five Pillars. The other dimension they provide is balance, which in effect almost automatically follows from applying the Five Pillars. You'll find that they also provide a common language for all stakeholders, both in the IT and business domains.

This very high-level review has probably led you to ask a number of key questions such as:

- ➤ How does the process get organized?
- ➤ Does it mean a new layer of bureaucracy?
- ➤ Can this work in our current organizational structure?

These are good questions, and how you address them will determine your success in achieving value from your IT investments. This is all about Process, the second P.

Chapter 3

P2—Process

In covering the first P (Pillars), Chapter 2 shows us *what* we need when assessing an investment. In this chapter, we'll look at *how* we put the Pillars to use as a process. This process is illustrated in Figure 3.1, in which we extend Figure 2.1 to show the components of the process required to deliver IT value through the Five Pillars.

I'll shortly address each element of the process, but first a quick run through to explain Figure 3.1 and show how the process flows. The Five Pillars are capable in themselves of addressing the myriad determinants of IT value when you work through the various standards under each Pillar. However, some Pillars are more important than others, both between organizations, and within the same organization over time. For example, a risk-averse enterprise such as a bank would apply a high weighting to the Risk Pillar, while an enterprise facing a cash flow crisis would emphasize the Direct Payback Pillar. We reflect this by weighting the relative importance of the Five Pillars, and we refer to this process as *setting the ground rules for IT investment* (Process Step 1). We have now modified the Five Pillars to reflect the business context (i.e., the foundation). Table 3.1 shows a typical set of weighted Pillars.

Having assigned the weightings, we are now in a position to determine the IT Value Standards. This takes us to the second stage of the process (Process Step 2). In essence, Value Standards are the decomposition of the Five Pillars into a series of standards or questions under each Pillar.

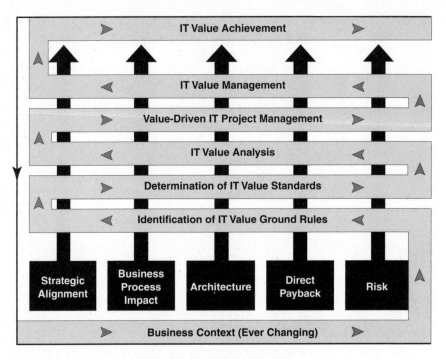

Figure 3.1 IT Value Processes

Every IT-based initiative of consequence must be evaluated against these standards before it will be considered for funding and approval. We refer to this evaluation stage of the process as the *IT Value Analysis* (Process Step 3). This in turn will lead to basic REJECT/IMPROVE/ACCEPT recommendations that also reflect the priorities established when setting the ground rules in Step 1.

Table 3.1	Sample Weighted Pillars
Pillar	Weight
Strategic Alignment	35
Business Process Impact	15
Architecture	15
Direct Payback	25
Risk	10
Total	100

For ongoing initiatives, this will inform us as to the current level of performance against our IT investment ground rules. For proposed IT initiatives, the analysis will show the value that we anticipate obtaining from them. I emphasize two factors here—ongoing projects and performance against the IT investment ground rules. I do so because of the importance of ongoing analysis (not just at the beginning) and the need to reference everything back to business imperatives.

The value analysis we have just conducted will now inform our investment management strategy. Do we need to replan or refocus our efforts in line with our IT investment ground rules? Should we carry on as we are? Should we kill seriously ill projects?

The next stage of the process, *IT Value Project Management* (Process Step 4), contains the core components of traditional project management, but a lot more besides. Project management typically operates on the basis of a stated objective, which is achieved over a given time frame, with costs and deliverables identified at various stages throughout the project. Value-driven IT project management takes things a bit further, for instance, by continually questioning the assumptions on which the original investment was justified. As mentioned earlier, this ongoing analysis is vital because IT projects have a habit of continuing to the bitter end even if the original basis has changed.

Ultimately, the IT initiatives being managed will exhibit a value profile that should be positive if the above approach has been pursued, that is, the benefits realization phase will be reached (Process Step 5). There is a further step that I call *IT Value Management* (Process Step 6). This is an important step because even when business value is achieved, there is no guarantee that this value will be maintained. This calls for ongoing attention to asset tracking, usage and inventory data, total cost of ownership, and similar issues.

Given the immense impact of IT investment on business performance, it is clear that the achievement of business value will in turn alter the business context in which the enterprise is operating (e.g., increased competitiveness, increased resilience to competitiveness, capacity to quickly bring new products to market). This, along with a myriad of other factors, will ultimately cause the business context in which the enterprise is operating to change, and thus the double loop is closed. The double-loop effect means using analysis not just to review performance against plans, but to question the validity of those plans based on this intelligence—a kind of postmodern approach to IT investing. This is represented in Figure 3.1 by the return arrow from the achieved and managed business value back to the business context.

To illustrate this, take the example of an enterprise that implements a comprehensive CRM application. This has significant impact in terms of reducing customer churn and increasing revenue through better cross selling. This modifies the business context for the enterprise, because both its position in the marketplace and its financial strength have been significantly enhanced. Finally, it is likely to alter business priorities, which should then be reflected in revised ground rules. This emphasizes the real-time, ongoing nature of our benefits realization process.

Now let's look at the steps in more detail. As we work through these steps, I'll refer to the roles and activities of a number of key governance bodies. While these will be comprehensively covered in Chapter 4 (People, the third P) it's worthwhile to take a very quick overview at this stage:

IT Council: Involves the definition of strategy and the setting of ground rules and priorities for IT expenditure.

IT Investment Board: Ensures that potential IT investment proposals and opportunities are thoroughly analyzed within guidelines defined by the IT Council and developing concise assessments and recommendations for presentation to the IT Council.

Office of Architecture and Standards: Ensures that corporate architectural and business value standards are comprehensively addressed as part of the assessment process.

Project Office: Brings best practice in project management to both the initial feasibility assessment (e.g., the project risk) and to the ongoing review of the project.

◼ STEP 1: SETTING THE GROUND RULES

We have seen how the Five Pillars of Benefits Realization provide a comprehensive coverage of the key issues. But the relative importance of those Pillars/perspectives varies between organizations. For instance, a company with severe cash-flow problems is likely to assign a high weighting to Direct Payback (particularly direct cash savings), and to assign a low weighting to Architecture (although it could be argued that cash problems would cause a high weighting on Architecture to minimize support costs). By way of contrast, a financially strong company, seeking to position itself for future expansion, would probably reverse these weightings. This is an important consideration because while it's vital to have the rounded view provided by the five perspectives, affording each perspective equal importance would distort the eventual findings. For the exercise to be realistic, therefore, we need a set of weightings reflecting corporate values and priorities. We often refer to these as the *Investment Ground Rules*.

When Gartner undertakes this exercise, we begin by asking senior business and IT management. Ideally this should be structured as an IT Council or equivalent to apply these ground rule weightings. The process usually starts with a strongly interactive workshop that aims to instill a high-level understanding of the drivers and dynamics of successful IT investments. (There will probably be some knowledge shortfall in that area.) This approach is strongly recommended, as is the interactive format. Executives often feel uncertain or even intimidated when faced with this task, so it's vital to get them feeling comfortable and familiar with the material. A valuable aid to understanding at the workshop(s) is to express the concepts in terms of the individual enterprise or vertical sector (e.g., financial services, government). It's also important to provide plenty of examples. If you confine yourself to generic principles, you'll face a room of glazed eyes within a short time. Once we are sure that management fully understands the concepts and their role in setting the ground rules, we ask each participant to complete (within a few days) the following worksheet:

Weighting the Five Investment Perspectives

Introduction

This document seeks to help Company XXX's management team set the ground rules that will underpin the development of the IT. It involves the assignment of weightings to the use of information technology under the five key perspectives discussed in the management awareness workshop, namely:

1. Strategic Alignment.
2. Business Process Impact.
3. Architecture.
4. Direct Payback.
5. Risk.

This is quite a brief exercise. Guidelines for the completion of the weighting table are provided.

Defining the Ground Rules

Investments in IT frequently give rise to disappointing results. The Gartner Group has developed a framework to help managers address this problem and one of the first steps we take is to ensure that business issues underpinning the investment are prioritized. We do this because, with all IT investments, there is a trade-off between elements, the most obvious being cost as against power and functionality. We have identified five perspectives through which investments should be evaluated.

When management has assigned priorities to these perspectives, we will then be in a position to score alternative IT solutions against these priorities, leading to the selection of the solution set which delivers the maximum benefit to your organization.

Examine each of the following perspectives, and based on their relative importance to your company's objectives, assign a weight to each of them, adding to a total of 100 (equal to an average of 20). Even though some managers seek to achieve great precision, increments of 5 or possibly even 10 are adequate. Don't worry if some perspectives seem to overlap. Remember that the purpose of this exercise is to establish in broad terms the business priorities that should underpin the planned investment in IT.

1: Strategic Alignment

This perspective refers to the importance you attach to the medium/long-term alignment of your IT facilities to your organizational goals. Typical issues to consider: Does the organization plan to alter its structure, change the manner in which it delivers its services, or have to rapidly respond to changing customer requirements? Does it intend to modify the culture of the organization, for instance, by empowering staff and reducing direct control? Is there an intention to outsource key activities? If so, strategic alignment between your computer systems and your corporate objectives is likely to be important. Another point to remember, if your business plans and/or prospects are unclear, or are likely to change significantly in the short to medium term, then this weight would have to be reduced, as achieving strategic alignment in such circumstances would be more difficult.

2: Business Process Impact

Does your organization require the capacity to rapidly and radically change business processes (a business process is any series of tasks leading to a stated objective) in line with changing business conditions? (This is particularly important in industries such as IT and telecommunications, less so in discrete manufacturing.) If so, you need to assign a high weight to this, as IT is a key enabler of process transformation. You may also need to assign a high weighting to this if your existing processes show signs of malfunction. Typical symptoms include capture of data more than once, inflexibility, long turnaround times, too much checking and nonvalue-adding controls.

3: Architecture

Your IT architecture is represented by your computer hardware, software, databases, and telecommunications facilities. Management often finds it hard to assign a weighting to this perspective, but it can be very important. A badly integrated architecture would mean that various systems fail to talk to one another, resulting in unproductive work and an inability to fully capitalize on your information resources. For instance, if you have a closed architecture, you may not be able to link effectively between departments or with trading partners, an increasingly important consideration. Some architectures can accommodate change well, others do not. Some may be headed for technological limbo, while others may be well positioned to accommodate and capitalize on new technological developments. If compliance with appropriate architectural standards is important to you, assign a high weighting to Architecture.

4: Direct Payback

This relates to direct benefits such as cost savings of any kind, cost avoidance, revenue enhancement, better/faster information, and other forms of immediate, direct benefits. If these are important to you, assign a high weight to this perspective.

5: Risk

All IT projects involve organizational and technical risk to some degree. Some organizations have a risk-averse culture, while others are more adventurous. Banks, for instance, always assign a very high weighting to Risk, because IT is essential to their very survival. Risk is not so important for organizations where a system failure, for example, will not result in the shutdown of key services. To weight this perspective properly, you need to ask yourself the question: What are the consequences for your organization if we invest in systems which prove troublesome to install and manage or which may suffer breakdowns from time to time? If the nature of your business is such that any level of disruption would have serious long-term ramifications, then you need to weight this perspective highly. If you assign a high weighting to Risk, the likelihood of the safe, predictable alternative being selected as against the innovative one will increase.

Your Weightings

Now record your weightings in the table shown. Remember your total must equal 100 percent. If you increase the weighting for any individual perspective you must decrease the weighting of one or more of the others to maintain a constant total.

Perspective	Weight
Strategic Alignment	
Business Process Impact	
Architecture	
Direct Payback	
Risk	
Total	100%

Name: _____

Position: _____

Date: _____

We have found that in such exercises, wide variations may arise in the weightings assigned. This is understandable because executives generally come up through an organization within a very limited range of functional areas. For example, you don't see very much crossing over between engineering and marketing or human resources and IT. Thus, executives will be inclined to approach an exercise such as this from a functional perspective. Another factor is that they often have experience of a limited number of vertical sectors. Inevitably, when a team-based initiative such as this takes place, difficulties arise. As a result, you'll see the CFO tending to favor Direct Payback, while the CIO might emphasize Architecture. It is essential that these differences be reconciled, not just to have a tidy document at the end, but to ensure agreement among the organization's executives on the strategic priorities that underpin IT investments. If this agreement cannot be reached (or even if it is difficult to achieve) on such a fundamental issue, the organization has a problem that needs to be addressed urgently. If top executives cannot define priorities, how can their line managers implement them? While this is fairly basic, I have seen too many organizations with this problem to not mention it. Most often the reason this happens is the absence of a clear strategy, or the failure to communicate a strategy that has been developed. Every organization will say it has a strategy, but often it is unclear and/or has not been communicated to the general workforce, even to senior management. I did an assignment in a company where everyone said that there was "no strategy." Yet when I raised this with the CEO, he indignantly denied it, and by way of proof, brandished a pristine document that had been developed by a leading consultancy company about 12 months previously! A clear *well-communicated* strategy is one of the first priorities.

To recap, the primary objective of this exercise is to provide a basis for reconciling the trade-offs inherent in any investment proposal. It reflects top executives' priorities and will govern all recommendations made by the Investment Board. Quite apart from setting the ground rules, the very exercise of reaching such agreement is in itself of tremendous value to the enterprise. First, it greatly increases the stakeholders' knowledge of the linkage between IT and business value. Second, it clarifies and/or reveals existing misunderstandings or disagreements between executives on strategic priorities.

Chapters 1 and 2 underlined the rapid rate at which business and technology are changing, and the unpredictability of this change in terms of scope, range, and direction. Despite the well-publicized dot-com crashes, e-business continues to make relentless progress, changing business models, and relationships between firms. These developments mean that IT has an ever-increasing impact on business performance and hence on executives charged with enhancing that performance. Consequentially, the exercise of allocating ground rule priorities for IT investments assumes a corresponding importance. Table 3.2 gives a few typical examples of translating business priorities into ground rule weightings.

Issue	Increase/Decrease Relative Importance?
Table 3.2	**Translating Business Priorities into Ground Rules**

Strategic Alignment

Issue	Increase/Decrease Relative Importance?
IT is not a major enabler of competitive advantage to this firm.	Decrease: The importance of Strategic Alignment is directly related to the impact of IT on the firm's performance.
We are likely to integrate more closely with important trading partners.	Increase: Such integration will be heavily dependent on IT.
We are likely to engage in a merger or takeover.	Increase: IT decisions taken now could have a significant impact on the speed and cohesiveness of such an initiative.
We are unsure about our strategic directions.	Decrease: There is little point in trying to closely align IT investments with a strategy that is not clearly defined, or could change soon.
We plan to outsource many of our operations, both business and IT.	Decrease: This is a rather tricky one, but basically when an enterprise is heavily outsourced, IT has less strategic impact.

Business Process Impact

Issue	Increase/Decrease Relative Importance?
We are likely to integrate more closely with important trading partners.	Increase: Such integration will be heavily dependent on IT.
We have undergone a BPR exercise and have rationalized our processes.	Decrease: Rationalized processes require less attention than those that have not been rationalized.
Our volatile market conditions mean our products and services could require significant changes.	Increase: This requirement will call for flexible business processes, enabled by IT.
Our core transaction processing facilities are based on legacy applications.	Increase: Legacy applications almost certainly mean legacy business processes, which are unsuitable to today's environment.

Table 3.2   Continued

Issue	Increase/Decrease Relative Importance?

Architecture

We plan to change our organizational structure from strong centralization to more independent business units.	Increase: The IT architecture would be an important underpinning of this initiative.
Our volatile market conditions mean our products and services could require significant changes.	Increase: This requirement will call for compliance with a flexible and adaptable IT architecture.
We are likely to integrate more closely with important trading partners.	Increase: Such integration will be heavily dependent on IT.
We have an immediate need for cash and cost savings.	Decrease: Architecture has little immediate contribution to this requirement.
Our organizational structure is highly decentralized.	Decrease: IT architecture assumes less importance in a decentralized organization.

Direct Payback

Because of our volatile market conditions, our products and services could require significant changes.	Decrease: Immediate benefits may need to be sacrificed/deferred to meet this requirement.
We have an immediate need for cash and cost savings.	Increase: Direct payback is the area to focus on for savings and cash flow.
Our head count ratios are significantly out of line with our sister companies.	Increase: Head count reduction seems to be required.

Risk

IT is not a major enabler of competitive advantage to this firm.	Decrease: This means that an IT-related risk would not be overly significant.
We plan to change our organizational structure from strong centralization to more independent business units.	Increase: Any such initiative involves an increased degree of risk.

(continued)

Issue	Increase/Decrease Relative Importance?
Table 3.2 Continued	
We are likely to engage in a merger or takeover.	Increase: Any such initiative involves an increased degree of risk.
Our culture does not tolerate risk taking.	Increase: This culture demands a strong emphasis, and hence weighting, for Risk.
Our business is now dependent on real-time data and interactions with customers.	Increase: The business cannot tolerate any failures in the IT infrastructure.

I used the example of "We are likely to integrate more closely with important trading partners" under a number of different Pillars. This is intentional because I want to emphasize that a business imperative can extend beyond a single Pillar, often increasing the importance of one while reducing others.

To ensure you have grasped the basics of these concepts, you should now define some ground rules yourself. Go back to the six case studies in Chapter 1 and, putting yourself in the position of senior management in each of these organizations, allocate weightings that you consider to be appropriate to the situation. Remember you are forming the basis for allocating scarce resources (e.g., money, staff, management time) for IT-related projects. When you have done that, refer to Appendix C and you'll see the weightings that I have given, and the rationale for them. Bear in mind that there is no right set of weightings (although having said that, it's often pretty easy to tell wrong ones!).

Review the case studies quickly and fill in the checklist in Table 3.3.

Always keep in mind that this exercise is a valuable tool for your management team even if it never came to be used as part of a formal IT investment appraisal process. It forces and encourages management to understand the factors that enable IT to create business value (and don't underestimate this as an

Table 3.3   Weightings Exercise

Case Study	Strategic Alignment	Business Process Impact	Architecture	Direct Payback	Risk

achievement in itself), establishes a common language to bridge the business/IT chasm, and also to set priorities in terms of resource allocation. This will be a new experience for many, if not most, executives. When there are wide divergences in the weightings, as there frequently are, it suggests that the enterprise is pulling in different directions. The process of reconciling these variances can be revealing. Sometimes the variances arise from a lack of understanding, but more frequently they reflect fundamental differences on where the organization is now, where it is going, and how it should get there. Trying to obtain business value from IT in such circumstances is almost impossible, yet that is what happens all too often as these differences tend not to become explicit in other management forums.

➤ Disseminate! Communicate!

One additional but vital ingredient remains. These ground rules should be widely disseminated throughout the organization. Every potential stakeholder should understand the thinking that governs them, and be given the opportunity to have input in the event of a disagreement. The best approach is to have the senior management team explain their thinking in a workshop-style setting. This would build consensus and bond strategic thinking with tactical plans. However, in my experience, you'll have your work cut out trying to get this done unless such a communication and feedback mechanism is formally institutionalized.

Step 1 has established the investment ground rules that reflect the relative importance the organization attaches to the Five Pillars. Essential as these ground rules are, they do not provide detailed guidance on how to evaluate and prioritize IT proposals competing for funds. For that we need to define IT Value Standards, and that takes us to Step 2.

■ STEP 2: DEFINING IT VALUE STANDARDS

In essence, IT Value Standards are the decomposition of the ground rules down into a series of questions or standards under each Pillar. By this we mean the definition of a set of crucial criteria against which all proposals should be assessed (see Chapter 2).

Standards provide us with a means of measuring a subject area against a set of criteria to determine whether the performance or quality of that subject area is acceptable to us, or to provide us with a basis for comparison to other comparable subjects in the same domain.

The objective of this step is to develop and maintain companywide benefits realization standards for business-led IT initiatives to facilitate their initial appraisal and the ongoing measurement of their business value. Their development is informed by factors such as the business sector occupied by an organization, an organization's business strategy, IT strategy, culture, attitude to risk, and amassed experience of successful benefits realization from previous IT investments.

How do we arrive at a set of organization-specific Value Standards? An example best illustrates the approach. Most organizations aim to achieve one or more of the following goals:

➤ Increase customer satisfaction.

➤ Reduce costs/avoid costs/increase revenues/increase profits.

➤ Improve product and service quality.

➤ Improve organizational agility.

➤ Increase market reach.

➤ Improve productivity.

➤ Increase market share.

➤ Increase brand awareness.

From the Gartner perspective, the measures or indicators that an organization uses to monitor its performance provide the basis for identifying its specific Value Standards. How would an organization measure, for example, the goal "increase customer satisfaction"? Some typical indicators in this area would be:

➤ Customer retention ratio.

➤ New customer acquisition rate.

➤ Customer approval ratings based on satisfaction surveys.

➤ Ratio of customer complaints to quantity of service/ product provided.

➤ Level of increased spend per retained customer.

Given that these indicators closely relate to a strategic goal, they naturally inform the development of standards under the Strategic Alignment Pillar.

Now we'll take Desktop Architecture (Architecture Pillar) to illustrate how you apply metrics to a Value Standard. The level of compatibility with preferred desktop environment might measure this standard. The grading is from 0 to 5, with 0 being wholly incompatible and 5 being wholly compatible. In practice, this could work out as follows:

Windows 2000 = 5

Win 98 = 4

Mac = 1

When we undertake IT Value Analysis (Step 3), we will have these Value Standards metrics to guide us in determining the desirability of the investment.

➤ Consistency and Balance

Inadequate and unbalanced evaluation criteria are among the main reasons for the poor return from IT investments. But a related problem has been the use of different acceptance criteria—sometimes dramatically different—that vary over time and between projects. In other words, there might be one set of standards used to justify an investment today, and a different set tomorrow. While I'm not saying that evaluation standards should never change, or that they should be exactly the same for each project, surely it is impossible to determine the respective value of proposals if the goal posts move each time. My recommendation is that they keep to the same basic set of factors, changing only as business and technology considerations dictate.

I recommend following directly through on the same format as used for setting the ground rules, that is, use the same Five Pillars to categorize the Value Standards. Some key issues under each perspective are identified for evaluation (a comprehensive listing is provided in Appendix A).

Strategic Alignment

➤ Impact on merger, acquisition, or alliance.

➤ Enhance supply chain positioning.

➤ Empower staff to undertake more valuable work.

➤ Make our organization more attractive to potential investors.

➤ Increase customer satisfaction and public perception.

➤ Support new geographical markets.

➤ Enable the development of new products.

➤ Reduce dependence on individual suppliers or customers.

Business Process Impact

➤ Support for more flexible work practices.

➤ Reduction/elimination of nonvalue-adding activities (e.g., unnecessary checks).

➤ Facilitation of a process approach.

➤ Adaptability to accommodate new business requirements.

➤ Capture of data once and at source.

➤ Leverage existing data.

Architecture

➤ Consistency with existing/planned architecture.

➤ Scalability.

➤ Stability.

➤ Interface capabilities (e.g., APIs, support for common middleware protocols).

➤ Widely used (e.g., to support mergers/acquisitions/alliances, skills availability).

➤ Consistency with the centralization/decentralization policy.

Direct Payback

➤ Direct cost savings such as staff and overtime reduction, reduced inventories, and so on.

➤ Quality improvement such as reduction in backorders, fewer recalls/returns fewer customer complaints.

➤ Productivity improvements such as higher sales per employee or less searching for information.

➤ Enhanced employee performance such as empowerment/reduced need for supervision, fewer occasions for mistakes.

➤ Enhanced management performance through better information, improved decision support capability, or reduction in number of meetings due to better information.

Risk

➤ Scale of project.

➤ Definitional uncertainty.

➤ Organizational preparedness.

➤ Implementation time frame (the longer the greater the risk).

➤ Degree of top management support and commitment.

These are representative of some of the key issues to be addressed when assessing the potential value of an investment. The list should be adapted to your own organization's circumstances and requirements. While it should be modified to reflect changing business and technology requirements, this should be done carefully to avoid undermining consistency and organizational learning. Predefined Value Standard guidelines should be in place for as many of these criteria as possible. It's easier to allocate standards for a tangible concept such as desktop operating systems than for, say, degree of top management support, for which there is little point in trying to specify a value for a standard. The key point is to ensure that the issue is taken into account when evaluating the feasibility of the investment.

Recommendations

➤ While the definition of the Value Standards is the responsibility of the Office of Architecture and Standards, the task must be widely representative of the organization. The standards should not be seen as unrealistic, and/or imposed without due consultation.

➤ Strike an appropriate balance between changing the standards too frequently (consistency and comparative performance are diminished) and too infrequently, whereby real changes in business and/or technology are not taken into account.

Following through the process, we have by now transformed the high-level ground rules into a series of Value Standards under each Pillar. We are now in a position to assess potential investments against these Value Standards, and by extension, the ground rules.

■ STEP 3: IT VALUE ANALYSIS

At this level we look at the key question: Should we recommend investing our money in this proposal? This is determined by the scores the proposal achieves against the Value Standards. Evaluate the proposal against each Value Standard and decide on the extent to which the proposed solution meets the Standard. We'll continue with the desktop operating system example from Step 2 to illustrate this. The Value Standards specified in Step 2 suggest to those evaluating IT investments that W2000 and W98 both have high levels of acceptability, but the Mac does not. It does not necessarily follow from this that a proposed investment based on the Mac must be rejected. What it does mean is that against this Value Standard the Mac-based investment would be allocated a very low score. Note that these Standards can and should be adapted regularly to reflect the changing business and technology environments.

Table 3.4 illustrates some typical scoring metrics under a number of the Pillars.

Table 3.4	Sample Value-Standards Metrics
Standard	Scoring Measurement Scale (0–10)

Business Process Impact

1. Level of business conducted through nontraditional channels.

This standard might apply in the case of a business seeking to implement a new channel strategy. The 0–10 measurement scale would be equated to a target dollar amount or orders (sales and/or purchase) conducted through new channels facilitated by the new investment. Cannibalization of existing channels would have to be factored in.

2. Ability of technology to cope with changing business processes (more flexible work practices).

Dependent on the specific nature of an investment. Would be measured using a scale similar to the following:

0—Impedes business process change.

2—Provides passive process change support (e.g., provides core transaction support but requires human SOPs for process definition).

4—Provides basic process change support (e.g., new forms and reports may be developed but underlying process model is passive at best).

6—Allows for configuration of some key process areas.

8—Allows for configuration of all key process areas.

10—Provides totally configurable business process support.

3. Support for predefined best-in-class business processes

The 0–10 measurement scale in this case would be dependent on the proportion of an organization's key business processes for which a best-in-class model is supported.

0—0%	6— 60%
2—40%	8— 80%
4—80%	10—100%

4. Ability of technology to measure process performance.

The 0–10 measurement scale in this case would be dependent on the proportion of an organization's key business processes for which automated measurement of areas such as effectiveness, efficiency, and flexibility could be achieved.

0—0%	6—60%
2—40%	8—80%
4—80%	10—100%

Table 3.4   Continued

Standard	Scoring Measurement Scale (0–10)

5. Ability of technology to support new organizational structures.	Particularly relevant in circumstances where an organization is considering downsizing or right-sizing.
	    0—Technology best suited to specific organizational model.
	    2—
	    4—
	    6—
	    8—
	    10—Technology proven to work for multiple organizational models.
	    Scale levels 2–8 inclusive dependent on an organization's objectives (e.g., centralized structure, decentralized structure, hybrid structure, etc.).

6. Ability of technology to be supported by internal expertise.	If the type of technology under consideration can be supported by internal expertise, then business process improvement may be achieved more easily than if external expertise is routinely required.
	    0—Even minor changes require external expertise.
	    2—Minor changes may be performed by internal personnel (e.g., form and report amendments).
	    4—Medium level changes may be conducted by internal personnel (e.g., process rerouting or role authorization).
	    6—Advanced-level changes may be conducted by internal personnel (e.g., business rules may be amended).
	    8—Significant process changes may be enacted by internal personnel (e.g., role redefinition, process dependency modification).
	    10—New business processes may be fully defined by internal personnel.

Architecture

Standard	Scoring Measurement Scale (0–10)
1. Level of compatibility with preferred desktop environment.	0—Not compatible　　　6— 2—　　　　　　　　　　8— 4—　　　　　　　　　　10—Fully compatible

(continued)

Table 3.4   Continued

Standard	Scoring Measurement Scale (0–10)		
2. Level of compatibility with preferred server environment.	0—Not compatible 2— 4—	6— 8— 10—Fully compatible	
3. Level of compatibility with preferred host environment.	0—Not compatible 2— 4—	6— 8— 10—Fully compatible	
4. Level of compatibility with preferred database standard.	0—Not compatible 2— 4—	6— 8— 10—Fully compatible	
5. Level of compatibility with preferred development environment.	0—Not compatible 2— 4—	6— 8— 10—Fully compatible	
6. Level of compatibility with preferred middleware framework.	0—Not compatible 2— 4—	6— 8— 10—Fully compatible	
7. Level of compatibility with preferred networking standard.	0—Not compatible 2— 4—	6— 8— 10—Fully compatible	

Risk

1. Organizational experience with major IT initiatives.	0—No previous experience 2— 4— 6— 8— 10—Successfully completed many similar initiatives previously.		
2. Maturity of technological area under consideration.	0—"Bleeding edge" 2— 4—	6— 8— 10—Tried and tested	

Standard	Scoring Measurement Scale (0–10)
Table 3.4 Continued	
3. Past experience of organizations from same business sector with this type of technology.	0—No previous experience 2— 4— 6— 8— 10—Many successful installations
4. Project scope.	0—Wide, difficult to clearly define 2— 4— 6— 8— 10—Narrow, well-defined
5. Project duration.	0—Greater than 66 months 2—40–66 months 4—16–48 months 6—7–14 months 8—8–6 months 10—0–6 months

➤ Business Process Impact

(Given the nature of this Pillar, of necessity, the respective measurement scales are more qualitative than for some of the other Pillars.)

Who does this exercise is covered in detail under People, the third P, in the next chapter. Following this structured approach will not only guarantee comprehensive coverage, but will also ensure consistency when evaluating other opportunities. For purposes of illustration, let's take just one Value Standard from each Pillar, and assume we're evaluating a proposal for a custom-built stock control and distribution application (Table 3.5).

➤ The Impact of Ground Rules Weightings

We'll now return to the potential impact of the ground rules weightings. A set of scores not reflecting these weightings—

Table 3.5   Value Standard Scoring

Value Standard	Assessment	Score Out of 10
Strategic Alignment		
Impact on merger, acquisition, or alliance.	Being custom built there are likely to be considerable interface issues in this event.	2
Business Process Impact		
Support for more flexible work practices.	While the design is scheduled to optimize newly designed work practices, it would be costly to reprogram for changes in practices.	4
Architecture		
Level of compatibility with preferred development environment.	The system will be based on Oracle technologies running under UNIX, hence, will be highly compatible.	8
Direct Payback		
Reduced stock write-offs (obsolescence, scrap, damage, etc.).	This application will largely address and eliminate these issues at a reasonable cost.	8
Risk*		
Scope of project.	Small to medium-size project, reasonably clear objectives.	6

*A low-risk project will be assigned a high score, and vice versa.

that is, all Pillars assigned the same weight—might appear as shown in Table 3.6. (Bear in mind that in the given examples I have taken only one Value Standard under each Pillar for illustration so there is no equation between those scores and those in Table 3.7.)

This exercise results in an overall score of 46 percent. If we amend this to reflect the weightings, the overall score of 46 percent increases to 58 percent, as indicated next, illustrating the importance of the weightings.

Table 3.6 Before Impact of Ground Rules Weightings

Perspective	Weighting	Score (Average)	Weighted Score (%)
Strategic Alignment	20	7	14
Business Process Impact	20	3	6
Architecture	20	4	8
Direct Payback	20	7	14
Risk	20	2	4
Total/average	100	4.6	46

But what does the overall score of 58 percent represent? Does it mean we should invest or not? The Gartner position is that there are no absolute rules in terms of figures; again it comes back to an organization's culture and imperatives. However, we do suggest the broad guideline shown in Figure 3.2.

You'll note that applying the weighting transformed the example quoted from one requiring significant modification to one likely to be a good investment. This shows the value of using the Five Pillars to achieve a comprehensive coverage of the key issues, and of then weighting them to reflect organizational priorities, which gives us the investment ground rules.

The process of assigning these scores must be undertaken in accordance with prescribed governance processes. In the next chapter, we'll look at the roles of bodies such as the IT Investment Board and the IT Council. At this stage, the roles of such governance bodies are crucial. They ensure that the review is comprehensive and balanced and that the scores awarded are

Table 3.7 After Impact of Ground Rules Weightings

Perspective	Weighting	Score (Average)	Weighted Score (%)
Strategic Alignment	35	7	25
Business Process Impact	15	3	5
Architecture	15	4	6
Direct Payback	25	7	18
Risk	10	4	4
Total/average	100	5	58

Interpretation of Overall Scores	
Overall Score Range	*Interpretation*
0%–25%	Likely to be a very poor investment.
26%–50%	Has some potential but will likely require significant modification before approval forthcoming.
51%–75%	Likely to be a good investment but may need some fine-tuning.
76%–100%	Almost certainly a solid investment.

Figure 3.2 Interpretation of Overall Scores

fair. It is easy for stakeholders with a given agenda to manipulate the scoring process to obtain a favorable outcome.

A number of further key considerations need to be addressed during Step 3, that is, at the stage when you are deciding whether to recommend a proposal for acceptance. These considerations are:

➤ Full life-cycle costing.
➤ Metrics.
➤ Complementary Measures/Portfolio Impact.

All three are important. When considering an investment, most organizations take considerable care to work out the costs for hardware, software, implementation, training, and similar up-front costs. But the ongoing costs of operating the application or infrastructure are far less frequently assessed, and could significantly realign the overall cost picture. Metrics and quantification are all too frequently overlooked, or measurements are made only of those factors that easily lend themselves to it. We need to look at Complementary Measures/Portfolio Impact because, as we saw in Chapter 1, there is no such thing any longer as an IT project. Instead, we have business projects supported by IT. Frequently, these will require other measures to be introduced to ensure their success (e.g., enhanced infrastructure to support an ERP implementation). The cost and organizational impact of such complementary measures can be significant and challenging, potentially to the degree of undermining justification of the project under review. I therefore recommend that these three factors form part of the process at Step 3.

➤ Full Life-Cycle Costs

Typically, when investing in IT, executives take considerable care in quantifying the direct financial implications such as software licenses, implementation costs, training, and (usually but not always) potential increased hardware and networking capacity. However, these are primarily front-end costs, which, over time, bear increasingly little resemblance to the real operating costs, which can exceed by orders of magnitude the up-front expenditure.

The importance of these and related issues is such that Gartner developed the Total Cost of Ownership (TCO) concept to address it, and it has now been established as one of the major topics among business analysts and IT professionals. TCO takes a holistic view of your IT environment and considers much more than just the assets on hand and their acquisition, it also addresses people, process, and infrastructure. (This is covered in more detail later in this chapter under Level.) Many IT professionals refer to these as the "hidden costs" or the "cost iceberg." These factors can have a colossal impact on the total cost of the project, way in excess of the original estimates. For example, although a desktop PC may have a purchase price of only $1,000, many additional costs such as software, technical support, training, installation, and maintenance can bring the five-year TCO of that $1,000 PC to more than $45,000.

Full life-cycle costing must be a constant feature of the exercise, from initial feasibility right through to the implementation and post-implementation of the project.

Recommendations

➤ Understand all cost components and the assumptions made regarding useful life.

➤ Build a cost model that accommodates monthly or quarterly budgeting (whichever is consistent with your governance processes) for the entire life cycle of the initiative.

➤ Build what-if, best-case, and worst-case scenarios.

➤ Each cost-component owner, senior manager, and the steering committee should agree, in writing, with the assumptions that underlie each cost component and what-if scenario.

➤ Have financial analysts who are assigned to the IT Investment Board role run the numbers for senior management and the board's approval process and for ongoing stage reviews.

➤ Expect the full life-cycle cost model to drive many project decisions (e.g., use of external service providers), vendor selection, internal staffing scenarios, and a centralized versus distributed model.

➤ Metrics

Despite Peter Drucker's dictum "what gets measured gets managed," few IT initiatives incorporate any meaningful form of measurement or quantification, even with very large projects. Even less frequently do organizations undertake post-implementation reviews to establish whether the projected benefits (even if expressed in aspirational terms, such as "improved customer service") have been achieved. Hard to imagine, but it's true. Some of the reasons given for not undertaking post-implementation reviews include lack of time due to excessive pressure (often running two systems in parallel), the assumption that if the original appraisal decision was adequate, the benefits would automatically come (how wrong can you be?), and fear!

When I asked the finance director of a major U.K. retailer his reasons for not undertaking a post-implementation review, he responded, "Terror—I dread to think what the result would be!" Though his manner was partly whimsical, it contained a lot of truth. Probably the main reason the review does not get done is just that it never has been done. Furthermore, many of the original projected benefits would have been couched in such vague terms that meaningful measurement would probably be impossible.

Let's return to Drucker—"what gets measured gets managed"; the corollary of which is "what doesn't get measured doesn't get managed." The lack of a measurement culture in IT projects surely must have made a major contribution to the poor returns they have generally provided in terms of business value. Revisiting the ZAPped Manufacturer, you'll notice that there were no metrics in place other than getting the system in on time and on budget. Nobody was accountable, and even had there been, there was no system of metrics in place to gauge success. Ideally, the implementation of a metrics regime should not be seen as a threat to or imposition on staff, rather as a mechanism to enhance performance and corporate learning. This is easier said than done. Implementing a measurement culture and process is challenging and fraught with partial solutions and misleading outcomes. This section identifies the challenges and points the way to overcoming them, and thereby increases the business value of your IT investments.

Limitations of Finance-Only Metrics—Again

Chapter 1 highlighted the inadequacies of conventional financial reporting systems at the investment appraisal stage. These included:

➤ Short-term focus.
➤ Inability to value intangible assets or soft indicators of value (a huge drawback in the Information Age).
➤ Focus on past performance rather than the future.

➤ Internal focus, missing key performance indicators such as customer satisfaction.

➤ Often based on departmental rather than process structures.

➤ A tendency to measure what can be measured rather than what needs to be measured.

These kind of limitations come back to haunt us when we try to measure the business value of our IT investments. This is because most organizations' measurement systems are based on conventional accounting and financial analysis systems. Such systems still retain the core elements that applied 100 years ago and worked for most of the twentieth century because the business environment was generally stable and product life cycles long and predictable. These conditions no longer apply and the clear inadequacies of these techniques have resulted in many executives throwing up their hands in despair and in effect making IT investment decisions an act of faith.

But it is quite possible to devise an effective, comprehensive, and balanced set of metrics when evaluating IT investments and managing the benefits. In their seminal work, *The Balanced Scorecard* (Harvard College, 1966), Robert Kaplan and David Norton showed how financial measures were but one way of looking at the total business, and introduced measurements related to three other perspectives that provided a balanced and comprehensive picture of how an enterprise was performing. A similar philosophy should govern the IT investment decision-making process.

The following are some typical nonfinancial metrics:

➤ Higher levels of customer satisfaction.
➤ Better customer retention.
➤ Faster response time.
➤ Lower staff turnover.
➤ Better staff empowerment.

While they may be difficult to denominate in financial terms, achieving these benefits would make a real difference to most organizations.

Key Measurement Requirements

1. Balance.   Obtaining business value from IT investments requires a balanced set of metrics. It is very easy to fall into the trap of providing measurement for just a few key performance indicators. However, just as financial measures can easily be manipulated (as in countless cases of creative accounting), so too can other forms of measurement. To take a simple example, a logistics manager might be charged with achieving a 30 percent reduction in inventory carrying costs as part of the benefits justification for a new ERP system. This target could be met, but perhaps at the expense of a sharp increase in the number of short shipments or stock outages. Similarly an on-time delivery target improvement of 10 percent might be met, but possibly at the expense of more erroneous shipments. Staff will invariably learn to play the system in terms of benefits realization unless the metrics are carefully balanced. If this happens, the numbers may look good, but there won't be a commensurate impact in terms of real business value.

It's also important to ensure that metrics and objectives are not conflicting or mutually contradictory. A simple example would be where a new customer support system might have to, as one of its objectives, increase the number of customer queries handled per day, from the current 30 per agent to 40 under the new system. However, the agent's focusing on this goal could conflict with the objective of making a corresponding increase in sales from the customer interaction. In such an instance, the competing objectives must be reconciled and/or prioritized. Again, if the investment appraisal process is undertaken effectively, such instances will emerge as part of the process.

2. Before and After Measures.   This is a vital requirement—without them you'll find it difficult to set meaningful targets for improvement. More to the point, you'll never know if you achieved them. You'll find that the exercise of getting current measurements is of value in itself. As we've seen, too often metrics are finance-based and do not take into account the broader business success criteria. This, in turn, can render the discovery of the broad-based *before* data difficult, because many will not form part of existing IT or management reporting systems. Nonetheless, it is definitely worth undertaking the effort to establish the *before* measures, even if it calls for a separate project involving programming or manual data collection and analysis. A key recommendation is to ensure that the new system incorporates the new metrics into its reporting structure after implementation. This is usually possible and will make subsequent performance monitoring much more effective and economical. By taking before and after measurements and carefully assessing the results, you will identify the Achievement Gap, that is, the difference between the current situation and the targeted achievement metric. The governance process should then ensure that the causes of success and failure are understood. In other words, the corporate wisdom becomes institutionalized.

3. *Quantifying End-User and Intangible Benefits.* Attempting to quantify intangible benefits, especially those relating to end users, has always been a major challenge. As the role of IT changes, benefits of the intangible variety have come to predominate. The range of potential intangible benefits is wide, with commentators identifying improved customer satisfaction, higher job satisfaction, higher product quality, improved communications, gaining competitive advantage, avoiding competitive disadvantage, improved supplier relationships, exploitation of business opportunities, and faster and/or more focused product development among the most common. While the scope of intangible benefits is almost limitless, establishing the value from a business perspective is more difficult. This results in such benefits being regularly omitted from investment appraisal exercises and post-implementation monitoring. This exclusion is often based on the belief that these benefits cannot be quantified, and hence cannot be cost justified.

However, this belief is usually incorrect. Most potential benefits can be quantified, it just takes a little bit of imagination. It also calls for a break with the traditional financial accounting approach to costs and benefits. Let's go back to the item, "improved customer satisfaction." In terms of measuring this, most people would probably suggest a satisfaction survey, and more or less run out of ideas after that. While a survey would be useful, many key indicators of customer satisfaction can be extracted from most transaction-processing systems. A more useful role for a survey would be to identify those factors, rather than a personalized assessment of your firm's performance. The following are typical drivers of customer satisfaction:

➤ Percent of on-time deliveries.

➤ Time between order taken and delivery effected.

➤ Percent of products with incorrect specification.

➤ Percent of deliveries to the wrong location.

➤ Quality of product as determined by number of warranty claims and/or number of stock returns.

I could name many more, but you get the idea. The great intangible of customer satisfaction quickly takes on a more tangible and measurable form when we begin to look at things this way. The impact of these measurements, taken before and after implementation, could then be cross-referenced against the customer turnover percentage. The issue of identifying and quantifying end-user benefits is particularly challenging and a special technique for this is outlined in Appendix E.

Some concluding thoughts on measurement:

➤ While measurement is essential, it does have some unfavorable connotations, and again I'd blame the financial focus for much of this. Measures are seen as mechanisms to control and judge people. While there is an element of truth in this, measures can be used to foster an understanding of corporate strategy and performance drivers that will enhance co-operation between business units and stimulate a forward-thinking approach to achieving relevant objectives.

➤ It is essential that those being measured fully understand the basis and rationale for the measurements. The worst of all outcomes is where it is felt that goals and objectives were set without adequate consultation or understanding of the issues. To maintain interest and relevance, it is also important to provide regular updates to key stakeholders. Having said that, avoid going to the other extreme where stakeholders get bombarded with statistics on a too frequent basis. The reality is that some metrics need to be measured very frequently (e.g., percent of on-time deliveries) while others (e.g., customer satisfaction) need to be measured much less frequently.

➤ Bear in mind also that, in keeping with our overall philosophy, not all measures need to be quantitative. Some, for example, customer or employee satisfaction, can be graded as high/medium/low or similar.

Recommendations

➤ Remember "measurement equals management" and its corollary: "an absence of measurement means an absence of management."

➤ Most potential benefits can be quantified, it just takes a bit of extra work.

➤ The measures must be balanced, or you'll get a lopsided result or participants will play the system.

➤ Be sure to take before and after measurements, even if it involves considerable up-front work.

➤ Where possible, build in the measures as part of the new application, or write an additional reporting application to provide them. The measurement process will tend to fall into disuse if considerable work has to go into providing the statistics.

➤ Complementary Measures/Portfolio Impact

As we've said, there is no longer any such thing as an IT project, only business projects supported to a greater or lesser degree by IT. Added complexity arises from the fact that few such IT projects are stand alone anymore due to the pervasiveness of IT in every organization today. There is increased systems integration, not only internally, but with trading partners as well. To deliver business value, IT initiatives must become part of a broader portfolio of measures, some of which may need to be introduced directly to support the proposed project, others may be ongoing.

Take the example of a company introducing a Web site to expand its market presence. The benefits of the project are deemed to outweigh the costs associated with the project, such as developing the site itself and purchasing a server and server software. However, for business benefits to be achieved, many other complementary measures will need to be successfully introduced. These could include the need to manage and placate existing distribution channels, redesign internal SOP processes, introduce new credit control measures, implement an interface to existing transaction processing systems, and possibly upgrade the internal LAN to handle increased volume. Soft issues related to people management might also be important, such as reassuring sales staff on the impact of the Web site, adjusting reward systems, and managing realignment of the unofficial pecking order that may occur.

To realize the benefits from this initiative requires that complementary measures be defined, scoped, and project-managed in a coordinated way. This can be challenging, particularly in relation to the following:

Competition for resources: When systems investments are based on the portfolio principal, there is always the possibility that components of the portfolio might simultaneously require access to the same resources that may be unavailable to all at the required time. Examples would be specialized staff, technical support, and funding.

Critical path problems: It is likely that many of the complementary measures will, at some stage, depend on other measures being completed before they can progress. For example, an Executive Information System (Measure B) might not be able to progress if the underlying data were not scrubbed and rationalized by the user departments (Measure F). A related problem occurs when a number of measures impact the same department at the same time, imposing an intolerable burden in terms of training, organizational change, or data preparation.

Business complexity noise: Business complexity noise refers to the difficulty in correctly attributing benefits to individual measures when a number of different measures could have had an impact on the benefits gained. Reverting to the example of the Web site, sales might have increased in line with expectations following its deployment, but other marketing initiatives (e.g., price reductions, advertising campaign) may also have been introduced around the same time, rendering difficult an accurate assessment of the Web site's contribution. This point again highlights the need for an effective measurement system.

Recommendations

➤ Make a systematic effort to establish all the ancillary measures that will be needed to gain business value from your IT investment. If you're implementing a core application such as CRM, ERP, data warehouse, or some other application, don't rely on the application vendors to overburden you with worry about such things. They might, but it may be at a stage when it's too late for you to pull out of the deal.

➤ Complementary measures should be priced and justified in the same way as the main proposal, and potential critical path problems identified.

➤ Try to explain the potential noise problems to those accountable for benefits realization and isolate the contributing factors.

The next step in the process is where the real action occurs—the Investment Board makes the decision whether to recommend the project. While evaluating potential investments against the Value Standards is the main part of the exercise, it will lead to unsatisfactory results unless Full Life-Cycle Costs, Metrics, and Complementary Measures/Portfolio Impact are brought into the equation. These additional requirements *do not* involve major additional work or bureaucracy. If incorporated as part of the process, they become part of the way of doing things. Whatever little additional time they might require is insignificant when related to the possible impact of not taking them into account up front. I have in mind the avoidance of bottlenecks, benefits not realized, project over-runs, and other awful things.

Assume now that we have made an excellent investment decision, covering all of the angles. All too often this is seen as "job done." But there is another set of challenges. We need to ensure that the project is implemented successfully, that risks are managed, and that benefits are realized. This is where IT Value Project Management comes in.

■ STEP 4: IT VALUE PROJECT MANAGEMENT

I have carefully named this step "IT Value Project Management" to distinguish it from normal project management. The latter has come to mean managing the project to meet original deadlines and deliverables—an approach particularly suited to a civil engineering or similar initiative, where the components, objectives, and outcomes of the project can be assessed with a reasonable degree of certainty. Unfortunately, this kind of certainty is seldom encountered in IT projects (if you'll forgive me for using that term). Rapid and unpredictable change is the norm in both the business and technology arenas, often to the extent that the whole basis for justifying an approved project is undermined. Yet, experience shows that, once approved, IT projects get managed the same way as others. That is, keeping to the project plan outweighs all other considerations, invariably with less than satisfactory outcomes. As well as the conventional project management techniques (which remain hugely important) introduced in this section, there are additional factors that will help your project adapt to changing circumstances and realize its potential. These additional factors are:

➤ Phased assessments.

➤ Assumptions assessment.

➤ Risk assessment and management.

➤ Phased Assessments

Changes in the business and technology arenas are almost inevitable during the course of every project and the scale of potential change is far greater when complementary measures are taken into account. As we will see under Assumptions Assessment, these changes, either individually or in combination, can fundamentally alter the basis on which the project and/or portfolio was justified in the first place. We also saw that once a project is approved, it is pursued until it is delivered, even when no longer meeting the original justification criteria. Constant assessments, and appropriate management response need to be undertaken for each project and constituent element thereof, starting from the sign-off, through development/implementation, and through the post-implementation phase as necessary. There is also the issue of risk. There are myriad problems that can beset IT projects. Risk in the broadest meaning of the term (that is, not just project slippage) should be assessed on a continuous basis.

I recommend a governance mechanism whereby approved investments are monitored on a structured basis and at regular intervals throughout the project.

The Staged Assessment should review the following at a minimum:

➤ Assumptions—are they still valid?

➤ Are the benefits on which the project was originally justified still relevant, or are changes needed?

➤ Risks as per the investment appraisal review and measures deployed to manage them.

➤ Schedule as per the project plan—is slippage evident?

➤ Impact of complementary measures—are any of these falling behind or failing to deliver in line with projections?

From the initial investment approval phases onward, resources should be only committed in accordance with Phased Assessments. Funds may need to be increased, curtailed, or, in extreme cases, the project discontinued if the Assessment so indicates. Other options include redesignating the project to pilot status, or simply delaying it if the occasion warrants. These outcomes seldom happen in reality, as project success is perceived in terms of keeping within budgeted time scales and costs rather than on benefits realization. Getting stakeholders to accept this drastic change is often a major challenge in itself.

Recommendations

➤ Recognize that attaining business value from your IT investments calls for structured, ongoing scrutiny, from initial feasibility through to post-implementation.

➤ Standard project management considerations, while vital, are but one element of these assessments.

➤ Assumptions Assessment

Certain assumptions, explicit or implicit, underpin every investment decision. Stakeholders make assumptions about markets, competitive positioning, technology directions, capacity to absorb change, risk exposure, staff morale, and dozens of other things all the time. The following would be typical examples:

➤ A national telecommunications (telco) provider faces competition for the first time when a deregulated environment is introduced within three years.

➤ A bank must immediately introduce electronic banking because its competitors are seen to be well ahead in this area.

➤ An Enterprise Resource Planning (ERP) system will replace existing legacy applications following the merger of two national utilities.

There are dozens of assumptions along similar lines that play a crucial role when decisions on funding allocation are made. But, we are now operating in a volatile, unpredictable business and technology environment. Many assumptions, therefore, will prove to be unfounded or no longer relevant after a project has been implemented, or even as the project progresses through implementation. Many of the assumptions may not be correct at the time they are made.

Take the second example, where a bank's management wants to implement an e-banking solution because their competitors are well ahead in this area. Underlying such thinking is the assumption that e-banking will provide significant competitive advantage. In the case of the bank concerned (this is a real-life example), this assumption was flawed. Customers took to electronic banking much more slowly and cautiously than was envisaged, with the result that the bank's resultant IT investments could have been far more effectively and economically deployed had the correct assumption been made. In the first example, the telco assumed, and based a major investment program on this assumption, that they would be privatized and exposed to full competition within about three years. Yet the full implications proved electorally risky to the government, which deferred the initiative for an additional couple of years. Had this been known originally, or had the assumption not been made, the investment program would have been much different and much more appropriate.

Even at the time they are made, many assumptions will be flawed to a degree. In our current turbulent environment, many more assumptions will turn out to be unfounded as time goes on. They may not be totally unfounded, but the ground could have shifted enough to suggest that the original basis for the decision might need to be revisited. With rare exceptions, once an IT project is approved, it goes on until the bitter end, or until it blatantly exceeds its time and/or budgetary limits.

You will seldom see a project terminated or even substantially altered because the original assumptions had been revisited and found no longer operable. Why is this so? It's all part of the malaise that surrounds current approaches to IT investment, the kind of things covered in Chapter 1, such as applying Industrial Age thinking to IT-based initiatives, and a hands-off attitude of executives to IT issues. If investment projects continue on their merry (or not so merry) way when one or more of the basic assumptions have changed, business value becomes a dream.

The list of potential assumptions is large and will vary according to individual organizations and vertical sectors. The following represents some of those usually considered:

➤ Full life-cycle costs and total cost of ownership.

➤ Economic, market, and sales expectations.

➤ Potential mergers or acquisitions, either of your own enterprise or of competitors.

➤ Technology directions and the related vendors.

➤ Potential changes in relevant legislation (e.g., competition law).

➤ Sourcing policy.

In summary, it is standard practice to monitor the progress of a project using a range of project management and fact-finding skills. It is equally important, however (and far less common), to continue to question the assumptions on which the project was approved in light of new information and the experience of those involved.

Recommendations

➤ At the very beginning, when examining the feasibility of any proposal, the assumptions that underpin it must be spelled out. These should be collated by the IT Investment Board and signed off by the relevant stakeholders.

➤ The assumptions should be clearly spelled out and quantified (even within ranges) where possible. Seek to avoid vague or aspirational assumptions.

➤ Make clear to those making the assumptions that this is a serious issue and that they will ultimately be held accountable for their input.

➤ Last, but most certainly not least, re-evaluate each of these assumptions on a continuous basis throughout the lifetime of the project.

➤ Risk Assessment and Management

The Value Analysis level will identify the risks inherent in the project and the complementary measures to be introduced. If the project is going ahead, it is assumed that these risks have been deemed acceptable. Every project will have risks, and the key point is to manage them. There are various techniques available for managing risk, particularly for those within the control of the organization, and for putting fallback measures in place. New risks will arise and existing risks might change during the lifetime of the project. The Staged Assessment process should be geared to identify and manage these changes.

It is critical to distinguish this concept from conventional project management. Traditional project management emphasizes keeping the project on track, that deliverables and milestones are met, resources and costs controlled. These are all laudable and essential objectives. However, to realize business value from IT, it is necessary to enhance these conventional tasks with the additional factors recommended.

The Gartner approach to Risk management is detailed in Appendix F.

■ STEP 5: IT VALUE ACHIEVEMENT

This brings us to the stage where we achieve the benefits from the project, in a sense what this book is all about, and, in a broader sense, one of the most pressing issues for both IT and business executives everywhere. If the previous steps have been followed in the recommended manner, you will be well on the way to achieving the benefits. However, there is one very important concept I want to introduce at this level: accountabilities and how they are handled will be crucial to your success.

➤ Accountabilities

I have referred more than once to the need to break from the concept of the IT project. This is essential when executive management views any project involving IT as an IT project. The resulting focus on IT obscures the reality that the IS organization will not operate the tools day-in, day-out once the implementation project is completed. Failure to deliver expected value will then be perceived as the IS organization's fault even though it has little control over the day-to-day operations.

Business value is created through a combination of tools and business processes. The IS organization may be expert regarding the potential of IT tools, but the users are the experts on what business processes work best for them with the tools available. As such, the users must take the lead in defining how they will use their tools to achieve their business activities in the context of overall IS governance. Correspondingly, the enterprise (and the IS organization) must view each project as a business change project with IT components. This simple change in terminology not only places the focus on those users actually able to deliver the expected value, but the project itself is viewed in its business value context. The only reason to invest in IT tools is to gain the business value expected and proper orientation is key. Without clear accountability, the business value of IT investments cannot be fully realized, if realized at all. It's as simple as that. Yet it is consistently overlooked, or more to the point, misapplied.

Look back on the ZAPed sporting goods manufacturer case study. We know that everyone seemed to do their job, the project seemed to be a success in terms of implementation time and budget, yet in the final analysis the company was worse off than when they started. Who was/were accountable for this disastrous situation? The designated project manager pointed out that the project had gone in on time and within budget, as did the implementation consultants. The vendors were able to demonstrate that the system was providing the agreed functionality and IS could point to the fact that system performance was reasonable, reliable, and stable. Again, who was accountable for the company almost grinding to a halt? To answer that we must go back again to today's fundamentally changed environment, the Information Age.

Let's look first at a common and widespread mistake. Many, if not most, commentators recommend a single owner (that is, accountable person) per project, the project manager. This is understandable but, if not handled properly, unwittingly perpetuates an Industrial Age approach to project management. Because there is no longer any such thing as an IT project, the emphasis should be more on governance processes rather than placing all the responsibilities for benefits realization or project success on one person. Again, all IT projects are, in reality, business projects supported by IT. Increasingly, those projects transcend not only internal departments, but external trading partners as well. The potential risks and benefits mirror this wide and complex spread. Furthermore, any IT project will inevitably interface with and impact other projects and existing applications (see Portfolio Impact). While there probably has to be an overall project manager in such circumstances it is unreasonable to expect any one person, no matter how empowered, to be accountable in any meaningful sense.

Here, we need to be careful. Accountability is absolutely central to the achievement of business value from IT as part of the overall system of governance. The emphasis should be on the *roles* that individuals and business units play rather than on the individuals themselves. In its simplest form, accountabilities could be stated as:

> Relevant business units are accountable for delivering the business benefits and IS is accountable for providing a secure, cost-effective, and reliable infrastructure.

Returning once again to the ZAPped Manufacturer, we'll look at some of the things that went wrong, why they went wrong, and how they could have been avoided. Great hopes had been placed in the ERP system to save on purchasing costs. This would be achieved by analyzing comprehensive purchasing, supplier, stock, and finance data through sophisticated business intelligence analytical tools in the ERP system. Improvements were expected in purchase prices, cash flow, inventory carrying costs, and administration (e.g., fewer creditors to manage). The reality fell very far short of this.

A number of factors contributed to this, but let's concentrate on two of them. First, as we saw in Chapter 1, the history of supplier transactions and related data had not been converted and loaded into the system. This was a major job and not feasible in the fevered working environment that followed the implementation, which was when the impact of the omission was discovered. It meant that the analytical tools with their trending, co-relation, and comparative capabilities would have to wait until an adequate transaction history was built up—a year at least. Given the potential benefits, this was a serious oversight. Second, the coding structures for part numbers and analytical codes had been assigned on a silo or departmental basis in many instances. This meant that Finance and Supply had different ways of grouping and analyzing material, which seriously undermined the capacity to focus on business value opportunities.

We now need to establish why this unfortunate state of affairs came to pass. The reason becomes clear if we go back to when the enterprise was first considering an ERP solution at the early stages of the feasibility and systems specification. The materials manager in this case would have seen a demo of the system; the detailed, comprehensive reports; and the brilliant analytical capabilities of the business intelligence tools. He and the rest of the executive team would have been suitably impressed. Encouraged by the enthusiastic vendor, the materials manager would acknowledge that great things would be achieved. In due course, he would undergo the standard user-training program and everything would seem to have been on course. This all seems reasonable so what else could have been done?

With the Gartner approach, the following would have happened at this stage in relation to accountabilities. First, the materials manager would be asked, "What exactly can you achieve with this?" No vague or aspirational response along the lines of "better/faster supplier information" would be acceptable. He would be required to study the situation and to specify benefits such as the value of additional discounts to be achieved from supplier consolidation, or the value of enhanced inventory carrying costs arising from better supplier performance analysis. If he backed off from the idea that such benefits could be achieved, he would have been asked, "Are you saying that with all of these wonderful new resources, the kind of things you always looked for, you cannot make an improvement?" He would be on very weak ground with this, especially if there was any kind of benchmarking program in place.

It's essential to have buy-in from the stakeholders (in this case, the materials manager) and to work closely with them in identifying opportunities. The IT Investment Board would facilitate the effort, providing expertise, guidance, and encouragement. In this instance, they would work with material management staff (remember, this is at the very beginning, even before contracts were signed) to determine how benefits could be achieved with the new ERP system. Stock obsolescence was an acknowledged problem with this client. Every year tens of thousands of dollars worth of stock were written off. To address this, the benefits team would first establish the extent of the problem by taking measurements. They might then analyze why the problem occurred. The materials management team should know the main causes, which with this company stemmed largely from the lack of an integrated component coding structure between suppliers and internal systems. In other words, the same physical part would be sloshing around the various systems under two or more part numbers or product codes. The consequent loss of control led to the obsolescence problem. The capabilities of the new system in terms of integration and "one version of the truth" would, or at least should, eliminate obsolescence caused by this condition.

In essence, the materials manager would then be asked something along the following lines: "We now know that obsolescence is, for the most part, caused by wrong product codes. We also know that the new ERP system can have the same product codes on all modules and linked with relevant suppliers' coding structures. So it seems that we can say, with reasonable confidence, that obsolescence will be largely eliminated within 12 months of implementation." Faced with the inevitability of this logic, and hopefully enthused at the prospect of eliminating this annual headache, the materials manager would agree.

The next and crucial stage is for the materials manager to be assigned, and to accept, accountability for the achievement of these benefits. This would only work when the materials manager fully understands what's required of him. It's not just a question of assigning accountability and walking away. The full ramifications must be explained. The materials manager must be given the appropriate resources in terms of manpower, training, analysis time, and an escalation process in the event of his becoming blocked or stymied (this would be part of the governance mechanism, see Chapter 4). The key message would be that IS has the job of ensuring that the ERP system operates efficiently, securely, and effectively, and that an appropriate infrastructure is in place to support it. The role of the Materials Department is to ensure that the timing and content of the output will meet their needs and that they understand the system well enough to meet those needs.

Under the Gartner framework, the materials manager could not have taken the approach he did. Namely, admire the system, agree it would do great things, take the training, and leave it at that until implementation. Instead, he'd have to take responsibility for ensuring that he was going to get what he needed from the system, in the form required, and at the time required. You may ask how he would do that, not being an IT person. An essential component of effective accountability is empowerment. The materials manager, either directly or jointly with his staff, would be given adequate training, time, and access to systems specialists to get this analysis done. He would have attended cross-departmental implementation team meetings where the implications of such things as coding structures would have been identified and worked through. Assisted by IT Investment Board specialists he would have seen at an early stage that the coding structure he needed was different to that required by Finance.

Both sides have good reasons for their stated preferences. Here's where our governance processes would come into play. The IT Investment Board would seek, possibly with assistance from the Office of Architecture and Standards, to negotiate an agreed structure. In my experience, an agreement is nearly always reached in cases like this and every effort should be made to find a resolution at this level. Sometimes, this proves impossible or too time-consuming. In that event, the IT Investment Board would summarize the arguments made by both sides, issue a recommendation, and take it to the IT Council for arbitration. It is possible that the IT Council would rule that the stand alone arguments were justifiable. Who's to say they are wrong? They are making a business decision based on the facts as presented to them. But, crucially, it would be identified up front that in the light of this decision, obsolescence would remain an ongoing problem and the materials manager would be absolved of his accountability for this particular requirement.

If all stakeholders were to accept accountability along similar lines, the very serious problems encountered in this ERP implementation would have been drastically reduced. The issue of accountabilities is probably the single most important factor in achieving business value from IT investments because the absence of governance renders accountability almost meaningless. In the final analysis, there has to be a quick, clear-cut decision-making and problem resolution process in place, one that ultimately will call on top executives to make tough decisions, many of which will have strategic impact on the enterprise. Don't be surprised if they try to avoid these decisions, but if governance has been embedded in your organization, they'll have no place to hide. Once the approach is seen to produce dramatically increased value of IT to the business, and it will, the naysayers will start to come on board.

Recommendations

> ➤ The benefits for which the individual is accountable must be clearly defined, avoiding vague aspirations such as "successfully deliver." Objectives should be defined on

the basis of clear business impact, ideally accompanied by before and after metrics.

➤ Accountabilities should be decided and agreed on at the investment appraisal stage, not during the implementation phase, and certainly not after the system is implemented. A key element here is the agreement of the person designated with accountability. Too often accountability is imposed on an unwilling staff member, inevitably resulting in a lack of enthusiasm and commitment, and cover-your-back mentality. In short, a guarantee of sub-optimal results.

➤ The accountable manager must be provided with adequate resources and authority to deliver the benefits. The benefits realization process usually transcends departmental boundaries, and a manager will be placed in an impossible position if authority is confined to his own department. There should also be a clearly defined escalation procedure in the event of disputes or misunderstandings, which, again, should be defined at the outset, and ideally be part of the governance mechanisms covered in Chapter 4.

➤ There must be a clear distinction between IT and business accountabilities. IT will be accountable for successfully delivering the appropriate technologies, infrastructure, and technical support, but is not accountable for delivering business benefits. This is the responsibility of the relevant business managers.

➤ A change management procedure should be put in place. It is inevitable that a project and/or elements of the investment portfolio and complementary measures will change as time progresses. In addition, some management and staff will leave and others be reassigned to new duties. This could significantly alter the conditions on which the original accountabilities were defined.

➤ The management mind-set must be changed. The concept of thinking through the full realization process, quantifying metrics, putting in place a practical system of accountabilities, and sticking with it throughout the program life span will not come easily to most senior managers. It is common practice for the initial support for the process to wane over time. However, if this happens, those accountable are placed in a difficult position.

➤ Accountability for the eventual results must be reinforced periodically, especially informally (e.g., "When the project is complete, our A/R days outstanding will be lowered by 8 days; right, Mr. Smith?"). Simple, casual reminders using the sound bites developed during the preparation phase can be very effective. This is especially effective with top management. The IT Investment Board can coach them on using the sound bites as reminders to more formal reporting structure. Such reminders underscore both accountability and value expectations.

➤ **Benefits Realization Time Frame**

One final point on this level relates to the benefits realization time frame. It must be understood that benefits will be realized over a wide time frame subsequent to systems implementation. In the immediate pre- and post-implementation phases, productivity invariably declines for a period. This is the phase where staff is learning the new system while perhaps keeping the old one operational, followed by a period of mastering the new system, and perhaps also a parallel run. There may also be a time lag associated with the integration of complementary measures, that is, waiting for the full portfolio to combine to produce the desired results. The analysis of value achievement should be seen in that context.

The main emphasis on this step has been on accountabilities. If you don't effectively handle this aspect of the process, you will not achieve the potential business value from the investment. It's as simple as that, so ensure it has high priority. When you have achieved value from your investment, you have just one more step to take. You've got to manage that value.

■ STEP 6: IT VALUE MANAGEMENT

It may appear that Level 5 should be the last one. After all, we have achieved the main objective, benefits realization from our original investment. However, the way we manage and control our IT investments on an ongoing basis opens up a whole new range of challenges and opportunities. To continue achieving IT value, it will be necessary to integrate procurement, asset tracking, asset usage, and service history data. This is the asset management process. As Figure 3.3 shows, its scope has physical, contractual, and financial dimensions.

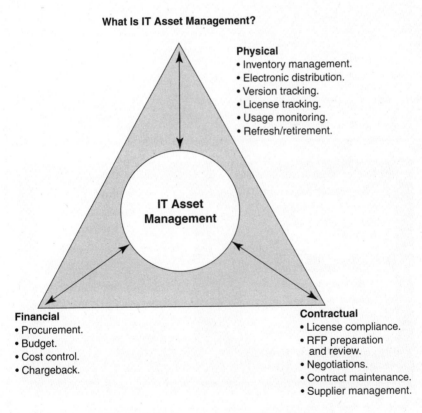

What Is IT Asset Management?

Physical
- Inventory management.
- Electronic distribution.
- Version tracking.
- License tracking.
- Usage monitoring.
- Refresh/retirement.

IT Asset Management

Financial
- Procurement.
- Budget.
- Cost control.
- Chargeback.

Contractual
- License compliance.
- RFP preparation and review.
- Negotiations.
- Contract maintenance.
- Supplier management.

Figure 3.3 Scope of Asset Management

Gartner defines IT Asset Management (ITAM) as the entire system of integrated management processes and strategies and technologies to gain control over IT assets throughout the asset life cycle. Just as with the investment appraisal and benefits realization process, asset management is a closed loop process that is continuous and improves with each successful iteration. ITAM can also be defined as the collection of integrated subprocesses and enabling technologies by which organizations (and their service providers) will continuously monitor the physical, financial, and contract attributes of distributed IT assets. It is a holistic activity involving elements of technology planning, business requirements planning, acquisition, inventory management, and, finally, disposal. The main processes

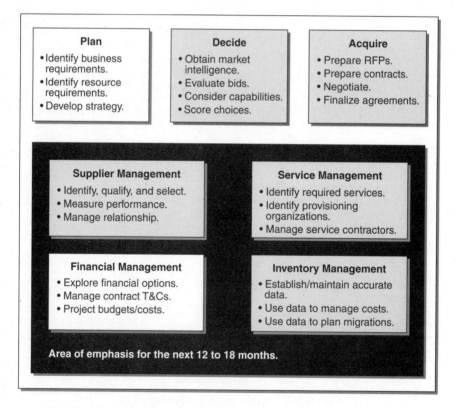

Figure 3.4   Key ITAM Process

involved in ITAM are shown in Figure 3.4, with added classification into those with strong business focus and those assuming greater importance over the next 12 to 18 months.

➤ ITAM Goals and Drivers

The goal of ITAM is to improve the efficiency of the organization and position it to take advantage of cost avoidance opportunities. It should also provide competitive advantage by accommodating mergers and acquisitions, rapid application deployment, technology change, and improved maintenance and support. Knowing what IT assets an organization has, what and how software is being used, and what will be used going forward, arms an organization with a tremendous amount of information that is valuable going into vendor negotiations and in managing those relationships on an ongoing basis. In addition, once a closed-loop process is created, including purchasing, help desk, and change management, the organization can better understand and manage the IT asset life cycle. ITAM data can also be used to determine if there is surplus equipment that can be redeployed or if existing equipment can better serve the business objectives of the organization.

Gartner research shows the following to be the most common drivers used to initiate an ITAM program:

- ➤ Lease management.
- ➤ Software compliance.
- ➤ Technology migration.
- ➤ Application deployment.
- ➤ Budgeting and planning.
- ➤ IT procurement.
- ➤ Property taxes.
- ➤ Maintenance fees.
- ➤ Help desk support.
- ➤ Mergers, acquisitions, and divestitures.
- ➤ Mobile device management.

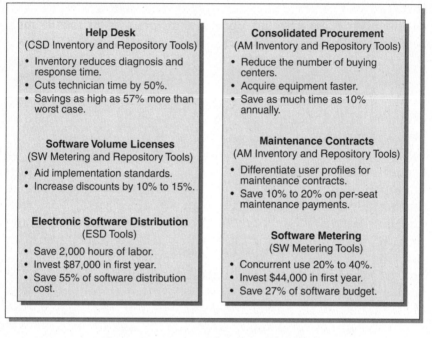

Help Desk
(CSD Inventory and Repository Tools)

- Inventory reduces diagnosis and response time.
- Cuts technician time by 50%.
- Savings as high as 57% more than worst case.

Software Volume Licenses
(SW Metering and Repository Tools)

- Aid implementation standards.
- Increase discounts by 10% to 15%.

Electronic Software Distribution
(ESD Tools)

- Save 2,000 hours of labor.
- Invest $87,000 in first year.
- Save 55% of software distribution cost.

Consolidated Procurement
(AM Inventory and Repository Tools)

- Reduce the number of buying centers.
- Acquire equipment faster.
- Save as much time as 10% annually.

Maintenance Contracts
(AM Inventory and Repository Tools)

- Differentiate user profiles for maintenance contracts.
- Save 10% to 20% on per-seat maintenance payments.

Software Metering
(SW Metering Tools)

- Concurrent use 20% to 40%.
- Invest $44,000 in first year.
- Save 27% of software budget.

Figure 3.5 Potential Savings from ITAM

Inevitably, however, senior executives will focus on the cost-saving impact. The good news is that this can be very impressive. Gartner research has consistently shown that higher levels of integrated asset and process management correlated to overall lower unit costs for technology (hardware, software, facilities, business resumption) and relatively flat support costs.

Gartner research provides support for justifying an integrated asset management system and process. Impressive costs savings are shown in Figure 3.5.

➤ ITAM Best Practice Guidelines

Effective ITAM calls for a combination of governance processes, tools, business involvement, and ongoing commitment. It is not something that is bought off the shelf or that can be implemented and forgotten about. The main elements are discussed next.

Hardware Inventory Management

This is comprised of systems and procedures to guarantee that hardware inventory data is up-to-date, with the data integrated into other IT and corporate systems such as purchasing, contract management, and back-end financial systems. ITAM should provide the data needed for the strategic management of the asset from planning through acquisition, maintenance, and disposal. It will assist in deploying the right asset, at the right time, with the right software license and warranty entitlements for the right cost and with the right service levels, thereby driving down procurement costs. This means you have to plan for disposal at the time of acquisition—not an overly difficult task. Doing this will enable you to purchase warranties that are not to exceed equipment deployment dates, match software application and operating system rollouts and upgrades, to negotiate organization license agreements, and to deploy appropriately configured equipment. This reduces the need to face ad hoc upgrades or unplanned write-offs. It will also help determine the appropriate service levels required to support the IT environment and plan for technology refresh. Most of this might seem obvious, but most organizations fall lamentably short in most of these objectives.

Software Inventory Management

This relates to systems and procedures to guarantee that software inventory data is up-to-date. Again, this data is integrated into other IT and corporate systems and processes, including purchasing, contract management, and the service desk systems. The software inventory is used to make purchasing and upgrade decisions. The main objectives of ITAM in relation to software are compliance, reduction of license fees, and managing total cost of ownership (e.g., distribution, reporting, inventory, procurement, configuration, and technical support). Total cost of ownership is covered in more detail later in this chapter.

With ongoing requirements to stay legal, software managers now face incremental tasks of usage analysis, Internet software delivery, and multiple application architectures. In addition to processes, tools to automate these tasks are required in all but the smallest of organizations. Additional assistance can be gained from deploying electronic software distribution (ESD) and software usage tools (SUTs). The latter, sometimes referred to as "software metering tools," do much more than merely meter application usage. They identify software usage patterns that include the least- and most-used applications, assist with license management to prevent overbuying or underbuying, and facilitate license distribution. Having effective ITAM processes and tools in place supports comprehensive reconciliation of usage information with inventory data and purchase records to acquire a detailed view of your licensing needs. Without usage data, you may be buying based on perceived, not actual, requirements. The potential impact of software compliance is underlined in the case study summarized in Figure 3.6.

Problem	Approach
• M&A activity clouded license compliance study. • Threat of an audit by FAST. **Objective** • Reduce audit exposure. • Gain control over software purchases and deployment. • Reduce software support costs.	• ESP recommended a multiphase multitool stategy, 800PC pilot: —Inventory using auto-discovery tools. —Map purchase records with discovery data using ESP's proprietary tool. —Reconciliation to determine exposure.
Results	**Benefits**
• Reclaim 1,165 unused licenses, saving $120,000. • Removed unauthorized SW, saving $500,000 and bad publicity. • Tools and process in place to track all SW purchases.	• Gained control over purchasing. • Used all available licenses before any further purchases are made. • Improved help desk productivity by eliminating nonsupported applications and corresponding shadow support.

Figure 3.6   Case Study: Software Compliance

Despite these significant benefits, many organizations have no formalized process in place to recapture and redeploy desktop software licenses when PCs are retired. Many desktop software licenses entitle organizations to use a particular software product on one machine at a time. These desktop software licenses are usually transferable from one PC to another. Therefore, when a PC is disposed of by an organization (and the software on the PC is erased), the organization retains the right to load a copy of the erased version of the software on a different PC.

Software licenses may provide discount leverage to future software purchases by entitling organizations to purchase software at upgrade prices, rather than the full license price. Although some vendors, such as Microsoft, are eliminating version upgrades from their software offerings, many offer better prices to upgrade older versions than they charge for new licenses. Thus, licenses have trade value.

Procurement Process

The procurement process (policies and procedures to determine user requirements, automate repetitive tasks, prevent unauthorized purchases, leverage the purchasing process, and ensure asset inventory updating) will be covered in Chapter 5. It's sufficient to say for now that IS groups should develop organizationwide procurement standards for hardware and communicate the underlying rationale to the departments, business units, and end users. Standards will result in better overall supportability, manageability, lower costs, and a greater potential to invest in and exploit new technology. Centralized procurement can result in significant negotiating leverage and savings, while decisions made at the departmental or business unit level often result in unnecessary heterogeneity and complexity.

Measurement—Again!

I've said it many times already: in business, we get what we measure. However, as in so many other areas of IT, organizations frequently do not measure their ITAM performance or they measure the wrong things and wonder why performance is lacking. This is a curious shortcoming, especially since there is no need to create a new performance measurement methodology for asset management. All you need do is adapt existing performance measurement concepts to the ITAM arena. For accurate and meaningful measurement, you need (1) a methodology and (2) a valid set of metrics.

(1) ITAM Measurement Methodology. Most measurement methodologies have three common elements: applicability, repeatability, and accuracy. In establishing an ITAM performance measurement program, we need to be familiar with these fundamental elements and ensure that they are considered in the overall design.

➤ *Applicability.* The measurement methodology must reflect the key processes that are executing in such a way that it orchestrates the basic activities, tasks, and outputs. For example, when measuring the ITAM function of equipment procurement, you need to measure delivery schedule, warranties, services, quality, configuration, and purchase price. All phases of the total life cycle need to be measured and monitored to provide a comprehensive view of the efficiency and effectiveness of the ITAM process.

By concentrating solely on purchase price, organizations may fail to consider other attributes that can be more critical. For example, delivery schedule may have a greater impact on a project addressing market share than obtaining a discount of a percentage point or two on the purchase price at the risk of late deliveries of hardware and software. Applicability considers process scope, key activities, and expected outcomes.

➤ *Repeatability.* For any performance measurement program to be useful, it needs to consist of a repeatable process that can be used to monitor key activities and identify potential problems. Simplicity of design is often viewed as fundamental to repeatability and should be considered in the design of the ITAM measurement process. However, repeatability does not necessarily mean automation. Manual sampling is a repeatable measurement process that should be considered when automated measurement is not available. Example attributes of repeatability are consistency of technique, documentation, forms, procedures, training, timings, and reporting.

➤ *Accuracy.* Accurately measuring a process is fundamental to using the results as a tool for improvement. There are several items to consider when addressing the accurate measurement of ITAM performance. First, precise definitions of metrics are essential to ensure that the measurement scope is uniform. Second, calibration is important to ensure that baseline and progress measurements are based on consistent scales and units of measure. Third, measurements must account for anomalies that could distort results and give false readings such as quarterly volume spikes or merged operations. Whenever applicable, these metrics should be the same as those used in developing the service-level agreement (SLA). An SLA is an agreement that sets the expectations between the service provider and the customer, describes the products or services to be delivered, points of contact, and metrics for ongoing monitoring.

(2) Common ITAM Metrics. *Cost* is the most common metric. *Schedule* reflects the time value of a deliverable item and is often the most overlooked metric component. When measuring schedule (e.g., delivery times and response times), ensure that consistent event-start and event-end parameters are defined, especially if measuring performance of an outside vendor or organization. Schedule consistency sets expectations; thus, consistency in performance in this category of metric can be more important than exceeding performance standards.

Content is the delivered item, service, or process output. Considerations for ITAM content measurement are items such as configuration, warranty, services, terms, and conditions.

Quality in this case is the consistency of, or expectation of, functionality or the deliverable.

➤ ITAM Summary

IT Asset Management is finally being recognized as a critical component and a barometer of the IS organization's success or failure. Asset management will continue to be a critical success factor in the capability of organizations to model, plan, decide, procure, and demonstrate the business value of IT. In summary, you should:

- ➤ Develop a software compliance policy to prepare for vendor audits.
- ➤ Track software use to prevent overbuying.
- ➤ Gather hardware warranty information to negotiate better pricing with maintenance providers.
- ➤ Implement an auto-discovery tool and a contract and change management process to recover leased assets, eliminate unplanned lease extensions, and prevent outright purchases to replace lost assets.
- ➤ Develop an asset retirement strategy to minimize tax liability, recoup software licenses, and recover any residual value in the equipment.
- ➤ Thoroughly review and analyze all vendor invoices.

➤ The Real Cost of Owning Your IT Assets

My emphasis all along has been strongly in the direction of benefits and outcomes from IT investments, rather than on the cost elements. This has been very deliberate, both because the business value is more important and more difficult to assess, but also because most organizations focus heavily on the cost/input dimension, hence the need for balance. However, costs are very important, and I now want to turn to a slightly different cost concept—the cost of ownership. This seldom, if ever, features at the investment appraisal phase, but it can have a huge impact on your bottom line and, hence, the business value you derive from your IT investments. The process should begin at the investment appraisal phase. Introducing cost management principles at this phase and continuing throughout the project will result in significant savings throughout the entire life cycle.

For this reason, Gartner has developed concepts that go beyond IT Asset Management. These seek to identify the total range of costs related to operating in a particular environment, additional factors that influence the costs (e.g., complexity), and, after the collected data have been normalized, produce a set of measurements that form the basis of a management action plan.

In the first instance, data are collected for the specific areas, personnel, technology, and employee and customer/end-user information. Components are further dissected to encompass costs, processes, complexity, service levels, and practices. The data are then validated and normalized, and comprehensive, discipline-specific measurements of the organizations are produced. These may include efficiency, productivity, complexity, costs, and peer average comparisons. The results can be used to develop an action plan for improvement of performance and cost.

This process can help us make more effective IT investments. Take for instance the concept of architectural complexity, which Gartner has identified as one of the main offenders. This complexity can be managed at the investment appraisal stage under the Architecture perspective. Using the Gartner modeling tools, your own data, and typical/actual values from our database, you can quickly assess the full cost impact of a proposed investment (e.g., migrating to Windows 2000). Complexity here refers to the variations in configurations, service levels, user dispersion, and other changes to the environment that add to an organization's technical or operational diversity. We have identified more than 30 factors as contributing to architectural complexity, but only a handful have a major impact on costs.

It's worth noting the top five "controllable" items, in order of descending impact:

1. Diversity of desktop operating systems and office suites. After organizations reach the point of having more than three to five separate OS versions (this could,

for instance, refer to different versions of Windows), support costs in terms of labor and connectivity rapidly increase. If you have more than five different OS platforms, including desktop and LAN servers, your support and connectivity costs (representing as much as 60 percent of the total cost of ownership of the desktop environment) may be 20 percent to 50 percent higher than necessary. Simplified computing environments cost less to maintain.

2. Maintaining a variety of different service levels also significantly increases the labor associated with help desk and break/fix operations. To meet more stringent service-level agreements (SLAs), the labor pools associated with support services tend to creep up in size. Greater variation in SLAs makes management of the environment more difficult, ultimately pushing support costs in the wrong direction.

3. The number of physical moves made by personnel in a given year will drive costs upward, and moving costs can be substantially more than just physically packing cubical contents and moving to the building next door. Server reconfigurations, pulling cable, and other nuisances can really add up. Rarely do moves of any significance end up trouble free. Consider employing a less physical virtual organization, especially if reorganizations are commonplace.

4. User dispersion refers to the number of physical locations of the organization's desktop user population. Although business needs may dictate where knowledge workers reside, any opportunities to consolidate personnel locales will likely pay off in reduced support labor costs. Generally, highly dispersed user populations are the most expensive to support. However, if business requirements dictate a dispersed organization, the organization may have opportunities to meet or even reduce internal IT support costs by aggressively seeking out third-party support providers.

5. Frequency of major software rollouts. It's great to stay current, but excessive churning of the OS and application environment can dramatically increase support costs, not to mention the reduced productivity for end users who must constantly become familiar with a new system. Careful planning of releases in an effort to reduce application versions and emphasizing stability of the environment can give you significant payoffs.

Reducing architectural complexity requires constant vigilance. If a 25 percent improvement (due to simplification of the environment) in items 1 through 3 were to occur, the average organization could expect a reduction of $300 to $500 per user, per year in support costs. There is clearly potential for dramatic savings here. You should build these figures and principles into your investment appraisal and benefits realization governance mechanisms, and continually assess and benchmark against best practice.

In conclusion, it is vital to take the total cost of ownership of a particular solution into account at the investment appraisal stage and to monitor it on an ongoing basis as part of your governance mechanisms.

Benchmarking

Benchmarking helps you continue to measure value from your investments. In the 1970s and early 1980s, we measured IT availability and system response times. Availability increased and response times decreased, but IT expenditure nonetheless rose to fund disaster recovery provisions and additional processing power. In the mid-1980s and early 1990s, we measured IT costs. Unit cost benchmarking became popular and chargeback systems were introduced. But service levels declined which lead to outsourcing as a possible solution.

You'll notice that all of these approaches suffer from the same shortcoming as conventional investment appraisal techniques—they focus on inputs rather than outcomes. As a consequence, current measurement systems generally fail to deliver the goods. Management needs an IT measurement framework that encourages and helps deliver cost-efficient and business-effective information services. Or, to put it another way, deliver business value. It's vital for top executives to see that IT investments are making a contribution to business success. Cost per MIPS or other such metrics are not the way, but that doesn't mean people still don't try. For instance, Gartner research shows that 60 percent of the top 500 companies regularly use such metrics to benchmark IT performance against that of their competitors. But such traditional measurement methods lack a business context. As we have seen, until now, measurement has focused on systems availability, security, or software functionality. Few IT measurement systems have ventured beyond the confines of the SLA. This IT-centered view of the business world has lacked any focus on business contribution and as a result the integration of IT priorities with corporate goals typically relies on indirect and informal communication channels. And we've seen the results.

■ SELECTING SPECIFIC PRODUCTS AND VENDORS

In helping clients deploy this framework, we are often asked whether they can extend it to perform detailed product and vendor evaluations. In other words, use it for product-by-product comparisons. The answer is yes. It can be and has been done. An iterative approach can be deployed when the framework is used for this purpose. For instance, the first comparative iteration, using more detailed Value Standards, might eliminate two out of five proposed solutions. This would be followed by an even more detailed iteration which might leave just two still in consideration or could indicate a clear winner. In one instance, a client used it down to a very detailed level to make a selection between the SAP, Baan, and Oracle ERP systems.

However, I recommend against it in most instances. The initial set of evaluation standards applied to a potential IT investment is based on the Five Pillars. As we saw, this focused less on individual products per se, more on factors associated with the organization itself, and the nature of the IT investment. Examples of the latter include whether the general technological area under consideration is mature, widely used in similar industries, the degree and nature of business risk that typically accompanies such investments, or specific risks associated with the organization's specific needs (e.g., very tight budget and/or implementation times).

Having evaluated the candidate IT investment under these product-neutral, but context-specific, headings, the organization may decide to proceed no further with the candidate investment or to consider alternatives that are better suited to its context before wasting the time and expense involved in evaluating specific products. (For example, an organization considering the full-scale implementation of a global ERP system may decide that the expense and business disruption involved in such an initiative, coupled with an unclear benefits profile for investments of this type in its business sector, is not sufficiently attractive to proceed with.) It may be better off proceeding with the integration of existing systems or the rationalization of existing systems into a narrower subset of technologies. Whatever it loses in terms of architectural cohesiveness, the overall investment risk profile may be more manageable and more amenable to the organization's culture.

Having defined the character of the required IT investment, candidate products may then be considered. This may be accomplished in a number of ways, using the framework directly. Gartner provides a tool for this purpose called Decision Tools for Vendor Selection (DTVS). This provides detailed comparative data between products and vendors, and is based on the Analytical Hierarchical Process (AHP) model.

Hierarchical decomposition, similar to that used in the AHP, is a proven, effective means to deal with complex information. It has been proposed and refined within academic circles and leading-edge businesses for more than 10 years and is now becoming a mainstream business solution for vendor and product evaluation.

The AHP consists of three steps:

1. Developing a hierarchy of evaluation criteria germane to the selection of choosing a solution.
2. Identifying the relative importance (weighting) of the evaluation criteria.
3. Scoring the evaluation criteria of each vendor offering in the hierarchy.

Gartner's DTVS and the related AHP model are ideal complements to our framework if and when approval has been given by the IT Council to invest. A more detailed explanation of AHP is provided in Appendix G.

As an alternative to the DTVS approach, organizations that utilize other detailed product comparison techniques can use the outcome of these approaches to extend the framework in a similar fashion to that described for decision drivers.

■ REFINEMENTS

We have just about covered the key elements of the framework, but when you start to implement it it's likely you'll need to address a few additional issues. The extent to which you may want or need to adopt these added refinements will depend very much on the culture of your organization, especially the existing governance processes.

➤ The Relative Importance of Value Standards

Just as we saw that some Pillars can be more important than others, so too can some Value Standards. Table 3.8 indicates how this could arise. While not wishing to complicate the issue, our methodology handles this quite simply by modifying the score allocated to the Standard by the weighting factor and then proceeding as per the basic process.

Table 3.8 Value Standard Identification and Weighting

Standard	Weighting (Out of 5)	Example Justification
1. Customer retention ratio.	5	A critical indicator because cost of sales to existing customers is 50 percent of that to new customers.
2. New customer acquisition rate.	3	Important indicator but, in current economic climate, we need to focus more on retention than on acquisition.
3. Customer approval ratings based on satisfaction surveys.	2	A lead indicator. Relatively important but, historically, has represented customer wish list more so than real requirements.
4. Ratio of serious customer complaints to quantity of service/product provided.	5	Critical measure. Customers complain when they have real problems.
5. Level of increased spending per retained customer.	5	Critical measure. We are far from having reached the saturation point with our existing customer base.

➤ The Concept of Probability

The forecast values for most components within a project are likely to vary from the eventual actual values. It is possible to forecast many elements with a considerable degree of accuracy (for example, hardware costs), while forecasts for other elements (typically, software development costs) are often subject to significant variation. This begs the legitimate question as to whether the value (scores) attributed to both elements should have the same significance attributed, that is, should they have equivalent impact on the decision to invest? The purists would answer no, but in practice stakeholders might be reluctant to get involved, and it is vital to avoid paralysis by analysis.

Table 3.9 shows a simplified application of probability based on the workings of the earlier example. It shows how the scores

Table 3.9　Impact of Probability

Issue	Assessment	Score	Probability	Revised Score
Strategic Alignment				
Impact on merger, acquisition, or alliance	(as above)	3	0.7	2
Direct Payback				
Reduced stock write-offs (obsolescence, scrap, damage, etc.)	(as above)	9	0.8	7
Business Process Impact				
Support for more flexible work practices	(as above)	4	0.5	2
Architecture				
Scalability	(as above)	9	0.7	6
Risk*				
Scale of project	(as above)	7	0.7	5

*A low-risk project will be assigned a high score, and vice versa.

described would be altered by the application of probability factors (0.0 least probable, 0.9 most probable).

Applying probability can have a significant impact on the final result. A simplified version of probability such as that outlined should be deployed. The difficulties of getting commitment to the investment appraisal and benefits realization process should not be underestimated and additional complexity might act as a turn-off. It depends very much on the culture of your organization and the way it handles change management. Few organizations deploy more sophisticated techniques such as the Monte Carlo simulation, even though it is a valuable tool for identifying the probability of worst-case and best-case scenarios. This subject is treated in more detail in Appendix H.

It's important not to get hung up on the numbers. The main objective is to go through the exercise in a diligent way, in line with governance roles and processes. If you do that, the numbers will look after themselves. Similarly, there is little point in worrying whether a particular Value Factor appears under the wrong Pillar. For instance, better customer relations could possibly be included under both Strategic Alignment and Direct Payback, but what's most important is consistency in following the process. The specific Pillar has little impact apart from a potential variance in weightings applied under the ground rules.

➤ Weighting of Individual Value Factors

This concept is very similar to that of probability, in that it asks: Should each value factor be attributed the same effective value in the scoring process? The method of arriving at the score for each value factor is very simple, just add up the total number of scores and divide by the number of factors. But it can be argued that some factors are more important than others. Take the first two factors from the Strategic Alignment Pillar. These are:

➤ Impact on merger, acquisition, or alliance.

➤ Enhance supply chain positioning.

The approach up to now would attribute the same significance to each (total score value divided by number of factors), but that may not accurately represent the real situation. Many enterprises have an active policy of growth by acquisition, often followed by closely integrating the new acquisition. The same enterprise might have a dominant position in the supply chain, which therefore is of little concern to its management. It could therefore be argued that each factor should also be weighted to accurately reflect this reality.

My view on this would be the same as for probability. It would depend on culture, commitment, strength of governance processes, and so forth. In reality, it would not add much complexity and would definitely enrich the analysis. However, perception might prove stronger than reality, so use it with caution.

■ SENSITIVITY ANALYSIS

Sensitivity analysis, a technique applied to optimize the prospects of a successful investment, is frequently used in the investment process and has been described by some observers as the most common technique for measuring risks and robustness. Sensitivity analysis in this context can be defined as an assessment that identifies the factors having the greatest impact on its success. Sales volumes, return on investment, and revenue protection are typical subjects for sensitivity analysis, but recommended only for large projects. Typically, sensitivity analysis involves assigning a number of possible outcomes to the key variables and recalculating the investment appraisal for each of the assigned values. This may identify vulnerabilities not evident by way of standard calculations.

Whereas formal sensitivity analysis techniques are easily understood and equally easy to apply (all that is required is the assignation of a series of different values to key variables, and a recalculation of the appraisal), it does suffer from drawbacks.

For example, sensitivity analysis:

➤ Can deal with only one variable at a time, whereas in reality nothing varies in isolation. This is a serious limitation.

➤ Does not show the likelihood of the outcomes, that is, the probability.

➤ Does not readily show how flexibility can be applied to minimize risks or exploit opportunities.

The formal application of sensitivity analysis techniques, mainly through its limitation to one factor at a time, does suffer from serious drawbacks. Nonetheless, the objective of the technique, identifying key factors and their potential impact under different conditions, is a valid one.

Should different appraisal methods be applied to different investment types? Many researchers and practitioners have proposed methodologies or approaches particularly applicable to different forms of investment, such as infrastructure or strategic investments. Many take the view that attempts to evaluate all investment types with the same technique are futile. Much of the opposition to the single standard stems from the assumption that such approaches are usually finance-oriented and therefore inadequate. When this is the reason, I am in agreement. However, there is no logical reason why the single standard has to be finance-based, but it can be, and has been, successfully applied in practice.

This still leaves open the question of whether one standard approach is the best. Once the finance-only misrepresentation has been removed, there do not seem to be strong grounds remaining to reject standardization.

There are a large number of factors, however, to support standardization, including:

➤ It provides a consistent platform on which competing projects can be evaluated (this an important requirement for investment fund allocation).

➤ It provides transparent evidence of fairness in resource allocation.

➤ It facilitates a comparison of actual results achieved between projects.

➤ It enables the IT Council to gain comfort and understanding of the methodology through constant use.

➤ It is almost a truism to say that management is reluctant to apply unfamiliar techniques. The practice of introducing different techniques for different investments would generate an even greater adverse reaction.

➤ The possibility of building a store of corporate wisdom for application in later appraisals is reduced when non-standard techniques are applied.

■ INVESTMENT SCOPE

As we enter Era IV, ring-fencing the scope of an investment becomes more difficult. Essentially, the issue is this: If a system grows and evolves during its lifetime, adding new and unanticipated functionality, spreading into different areas of the business, and providing core data for other unrelated applications (such as end-user computing), how can it be evaluated in an effective way? There is no simple answer.

It is more meaningful to address the problem from the opposite perspective. That is, given that there is no perfect solution, does this mean that the attempt to apply a structured framework should be abandoned? A framework that addresses all factors other than this must be better than a totally nonstructured approach, particularly if this limitation is kept in mind during the evaluation process. This is borne out by Gartner research and that in the academic sphere, which shows that the lack of an appraisal framework has contributed to poor payback, and/or that the use of a structured approach improves payback. While this factor, to an extent, undermines the intellectual purity of structured calculations, the limitations are outweighed by the proven gains from a structured approach, particularly when they are explicitly recognized during the course of the appraisal exercise.

■ SUMMARY

The weighting and scoring mechanism described in this chapter does have some shortcomings, but IT benefits realization never will be an exact science. When the process is developed through consensus between the business and technology domains of the organization, the result is an effective and nonbureaucratic benefits realization mechanism. This does not seek to minimize the necessity to tie down intangible benefits and costs in financial terms wherever possible, but attempting to quantify all the impacts of an IT investment in financial terms alone will give seriously misleading results.

The necessity for sensitivity and probability analyses is less clear-cut. Yet, these concepts can have a significant impact on the outcome of an evaluation and should be incorporated where possible.

When undertaken in the context of good governance, the exercise will not only optimize the chances of achieving business value from IT investments, but will enhance communication and understanding within your organization and act as a tool for both strategic and operational control. Providing rigorously applied double-loop feedback, it will act as an enabler of corporate knowledge and process best practice. One of the reasons for the success of the framework is that it can be adapted to each industry/vertical sector and to each organization or enterprise. It can—and must—be modified to reflect changing circumstances, either sectoral or specific to your organization. All IT investment decisions are shrouded in risk and uncertainty. Applying this methodology can reduce both the risk and uncertainty and help you obtain that elusive goal, business value from IT.

Chapter 4

P3—People

In this chapter we look at the third P—People—the way they act and interact. People are central to the achievement of benefits from IT investments. They need the best tools and techniques, but also a set of principles that determine the way decisions get made and conflicts get resolved at all levels, from senior management to technicians, within traditional hierarchies, and across business boundaries. Gartner refers to such a set of principles as *governance*.

Typical governance issues include:

➤ Strategy.
➤ Priority setting.
➤ Funding sources and levels.
➤ Allocating resources.
➤ Organization roles and responsibilities.
➤ Standards, practices, and guidelines.
➤ Autonomy versus common or shared resources, such as infrastructure.

Reading this you might think that it is nothing new, everyone does that. These issues are addressed in almost every organization in one form or another, but generally the way these issues are practiced does not represent effective governance. Too often decision making takes place in the context of rigid departmental "silos" that are unable to meet the requirements of today's dynamic, volatile technology and business environments. Without effective governance, people will take shortcuts, the loudest voice will win the day, ad hoc decisions will be made, accountabilities lost, and lessons from successes and failures will not become part of corporate wisdom.

Some of the case studies we looked at in Chapter 1 illustrate the issues very well. The problems encountered would not have occurred had good governance been in place. Think back for instance to the Gung-Ho CEO. He cut through the "red tape" (as he would have seen it) and took it on himself to commission a cost-saving product handling application. He had done a great job until then in cutting operating costs, so how would this be any different? But as we saw, the system had to be abandoned after a relatively short time in operation due to business process impact and problems related to systems integration and scalability. The CEO was assuredly the "loudest voice," shortcuts were taken and, as so often happens with IT projects, accountabilities were assigned only when a scapegoat for the failure was required. Effective governance would have ensured that the factors that caused the failure would have been highlighted before the decision had been taken. And, had the CEO still gone ahead, the accountability for the failure would have been clearly identified (if not admitted!). Take the case of the "Secretive Bank," where the Board made a decision with massive ramifications for IT, yet IT staff were out of the loop until the very end, resulting in the abandonment of a major data warehousing project. As we'll see, there is no way that would have happened had good governance been established.

It's essential, therefore, to forge appropriate and culturally consistent IT governance among business and IT executives in order to address the people factor. Rather than manage every IT decision as a new job, and make decisions on an ad hoc basis, the enterprise needs a governance structure that encourages best practices, and merges stakeholders' sometimes conflicting objectives for the common good.

While clear governance roles and processes are required for the effective management of IT across so many stakeholders, the solution also requires the acceptance of responsibility for participating in and maintaining them throughout the organization. Governance brings these key stakeholders together with a common purpose performed over time, namely to define the roles, responsibilities, and interrelationships among IT stakeholders within the enterprise. Despite the need to accommodate this large and diverse number of stakeholders, it is important not to "overcook the cake," that is, try to include everyone. If this happens, the governance structures become unworkable. The trick is to include a manageable number of key representatives, who are respected by their peers, and who are committed to getting governance working. Governance depends on the establishment of a partnership and trust among these stakeholders. This takes time to establish, and takes considerable "care and feeding" to maintain.

■ ROLES—A FOUNDATION STONE OF EFFECTIVE GOVERNANCE

The traditional type of organization doesn't support communications well across functions, particularly if new technologies or processes are driving change—and that is exactly what is happening today. As a result, it is common to have separate organizations for each application set (i.e., in a bank this could be loans, deposits, treasury, credit cards) as well as separate systems groups (e.g., S/390, Unix, and NT), each with a full compliment of skills. This type of organization is best suited to a static, relatively unchanging IT environment. Typically, these organizations are slow to change, and slow to respond to the need for IT innovation, but are strong in delivering functionally aligned services. Given the current rate of change, this organizational structure is no longer suitable.

To address and manage these difficulties, Gartner introduced the role-based organization model in 1996. It is based on the premise that there is no single correct organization chart, but rather organization structure is derived from the uses to which people are being put. In other words, the roles they undertake. It attempts to solve several problems that are common to many of the organizational issues referred to earlier, and which make investing in IT such a hazardous undertaking. A role orientation therefore breaks up IT support requirements into a grouping of capabilities that can be fulfilled in several ways, including teams, specialty centers, and by individuals assuming more than one function. The emphasis is on communications, process, and governance.

Key Characteristics of Roles

➤ The focus is on "what problem needs to be solved?" rather than on departmental or organizational structures and hierarchical working relationships.

➤ Role-based organizations look at processes and outcomes as distinct from "doing my job."

➤ They are cross-functional by nature, a "virtual" matrix that recognizes that organizational structures need to be mixed (e.g., teams, competency centers, and hierarchies) to achieve complex results, and that the organization's structure is a temporary holding place that must be flexible enough to change as business conditions dictate.

➤ A "role" can be undertaken by a group or an individual. For example, the Investment Board discussed later in this chapter undertakes a role, yet may be comprised of individuals from different departments and business units operating in a "virtual" capacity on a part-time basis.

The following roles—or their equivalents—are vital in achieving business value from IT investment (discussed in more detail later in this chapter):

The IT Council Role: Involves the definition of strategy, and the setting of ground rules and priorities for IT expenditure.

The IT Investment Board Role: Ensures that potential IT investment proposals and opportunities are thoroughly analyzed within guidelines defined by the IT Council. Develops concise assessments and recommendations for presentation to the IT Council.

The Office of Architecture and Standards Role: Ensures that corporate architectural and business value standards are comprehensively addressed as part of the assessment process.

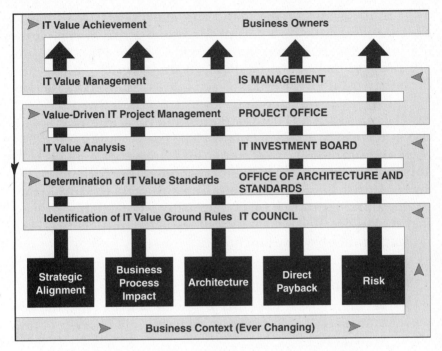

Figure 4.1 The People: Benefits Realization Roles

The Project Office Role: Brings best practice in project management to both the initial feasibility assessment (e.g., the project risk) and to the ongoing review of the project.

Figure 4.1 is an "updated" version of Figure 3.1. It shows where the roles come into play in the process. We'll look at these in greater detail later in this chapter.

■ THE IT COUNCIL

The IT Council, sometimes called a business/technology council or steering committee, assumes a coordination between the CIO and his peers in the business. It is the highest level IT decision-making body. The main objective of the IT Council is to provide a forum for the enterprise view to be discussed and evaluated, resolve questions of enterprise importance, empower the tactical execution of its policies and decisions through governance structures, and reconcile conflicts that lower management levels cannot. It analyzes critical IT issues such as IT investments and their alignment with the enterprise's strategic plan, risk, the overall IT funding level, infrastructure investments, and competitive issues solvable by IT. The IT Council takes responsibility for energizing an enterprise IT strategy, delegating authority to execute that strategy, and keeping it on course using a governance process that makes detailed decisions and resolves conflicts.

Important objectives include:

➤ Developing strategic planning guidelines.

➤ Resolving issues of enterprisewide impact (e.g., the balance between desired service levels and the cost to provide them).

➤ Setting of ground rules that govern IT investments.

➤ Prioritizing large-scale business process, infrastructure, and cross-business application projects.

➤ Allocating funds and resources for IT initiatives.

➤ Managing organizational change.

➤ Ensuring involvement, commitment, and acceptance of responsibility for the success of the critical IT investments across the enterprise.

➤ Empowering the execution of its policies and decisions.

➤ Monitoring IT performance metrics and benchmarking.

➤ Determining sourcing policy.

➤ Formalizing governance that lays down the roles and processes for the IT management model.

➤ Reconciling conflicts that the lower management levels of the organization cannot (e.g., contention between business units for scarce resources, governance disagreements, or requests for unplanned large-scale projects).

As these roles make clear, the IT Council acts as final arbiter when it comes to allocating resources to a project.

The IT Council serves as a forum for discussion between distinct business units or functions. It allows the enterprise view to be evaluated, along with business-specific requirements. It also creates a launch point for the requesting of resources and for those requests to be converted into actionable activities. The primary success factor in establishing a structure of this sort is the existence of a governance process or contract within which each of the participants can work.

■ THE IT INVESTMENT BOARD

The IT Investment Board has the primary objective of evaluating proposed IT investments in the context of predetermined acceptance criteria (these criteria, crucial to the success of all investments, are discussed later) and assessing the business case. Important factors include:

➤ Choosing the participants for the business case analysis.

➤ Defining the problem.

➤ Identifying the primary point of view of the key project stakeholders.

➤ Talking to users to create the best metrics, documenting their rationale, and gaining agreement.

➤ Ensuring that stakeholders in the process have all the necessary material, information, and resources required to effectively play their designated role.

➤ Resolving differences and building consensus on the way.

➤ Developing recommendations for the IT Council that are understandable and succinct (senior executives hate wading through reams of paper).

➤ Closely linking criteria to decision participants to ensure thoroughness and balance in the analysis.

➤ Identifying accountabilities.

➤ Ongoing monitoring of assumptions on which investment has been approved.

➤ Ensuring benefits are realized.

Key questions for the Board:

➤ Should it be done? The Board validates the business case
or value proposition for new development in line with
predetermined criteria.

➤ Does it adhere to standards? The proposal must be com-
pliant with corporate standards, methodologies, and
reuse policies.

➤ Can it be done? Using Project Office input, the Board
determines if resources are available and if the project
plan is feasible. The Board also correlates cost, time,
and resource assumptions between the project spon-
sor(s) and professional project assessors.

➤ Can it be supported on an ongoing basis? It is critical
that the life-cycle total cost of ownership and other operational and support issues be evaluated at the investment stage

➤ Can it be shared? The Board should determine if innovation can be reused (is shareable), and to balance resources and priorities across business functions to
determine if newly created functionality has enterprise
implications and viability, and whether resources can
be shared and balanced. For example, as discrete lines
of business build the first enterprise intranet or Internet applications, there is a window of opportunity to
share best practice, standardize methodology, and reuse
trained resources across functional areas.

Where a proposal has not met the required criteria, it is
either forwarded to the IT Council with a recommendation for
rejection, or sent back to the originators, to address unresolved
issues. Approved investments should be forwarded to the IT
Council for review and ultimately for sign-off. However, there
is and should be no guarantee that a proposal approved by the

Investment Board will be approved by the IT Council. The Council has a broader strategic role (think of the Secretive Bank example in Chapter 1) and it is important that it not become a rubber stamp for Board recommendations. Such recommendations should be laid out in a concise and consistent format, couched in terms fully understandable to the business executives on the IT Council. The Investment Board should ensure that a benefits realization program has been defined, including, but not confined to, the following key elements:

➤ Clear assumptions.

➤ Metrics.

➤ Accountabilities.

➤ Phased approval assessments (in conjunction with the Project Office).

➤ Formal risk assessment.

➤ Structured input from Office of Architecture and Standards (as per the Five Pillars).

➤ Structured input from the Project Office.

We recommend that the IT Investment Board should include the Financial Controller, CIO, and key senior business unit participants. Additional representation can be introduced for specific projects, that is, from the business unit associated with a particular proposal, and technical IT staff relevant to specific proposals.

■ THE OFFICE OF ARCHITECTURE AND STANDARDS

This office is usually associated with IT architecture standards, rather than "standards" per se. However, this Office should be the custodian of overall corporate value standards such as audit, human resources, and customer service, even if only in a virtual sense. I'll come back to this in a moment, as it is an important consideration when it comes to developing Value Standards for IT investments. First we'll look at the architecture standards.

➤ Architecture Standards

The glue that ties enterprise information together will be the definitions, interfaces, and technology standards. A consistent, modeled view of the information, data, applications, and technology architectures will be critical to ensure vendor compatibility with existing standards, and will serve as an input to systems planning. The Office of Architecture and Standards is the repository for enterprise standards, including traditional applications and technical architectures, a data architecture, and emerging architectures of information, knowledge, and methodologies (e.g., application development, data definitions, and network design). A second role is that of a governing mechanism to evaluate how well-proposed changes, or those already in progress, adhere to enterprise architecture and standards. If a proposal is nonstandard or noncompliant, it can help determine the implications of continuing the development.

Ideally the Office of Architecture and Standards should deal with three sets of standards. The following list is an illustrative, but not exhaustive, set of business, architectural, and technology standards that are the domain of the Office of Architecture and Standards:

Business Standards

- ➤ Support for business vision.
- ➤ Information sharing across applications.
- ➤ Interface standards.
- ➤ Scalability considerations.
- ➤ Reusable technologies.
- ➤ Listing/delisting approved vendors.

Architectural Standards

- ➤ Information architecture—How information is used by the business.
- ➤ Data architecture—Which information is converted to data, standards for naming.

➤ Applications architecture—How data is used by the business.

➤ Technology architecture—How IT supports information use (networks, systems).

➤ Knowledge architecture—How business users extract information (data mining, warehouse, decision support systems).

Technology Standards

➤ Equipment standards (platforms, operating systems).

➤ WAN and LAN standards (hardware/software).

➤ Office automation standards (hardware/software).

➤ Database tools and repository standards.

➤ Programming languages and development tools.

➤ Overall applications framework.

➤ Electronic commerce and e-mail.

➤ Workgroup and workflow.

➤ Middleware and connectivity.

➤ Data interoperability.

➤ Configuration standards.

Even though architecture standards have just been covered in some detail, the commonest standards by which the business judges investments, and is itself judged, are those of the financial variety. These include revenue growth, cost savings, return on investment, and market valuation. Everybody understands such standards, and what's more, they are very easily measured—the accounting systems are there for that precise reason. There are also well-recognized financial standards bodies, such as the Financial Accounting Standards Board in the United States, and other financial authorities around the world. Other forms of standards measurement have always been deemed somewhat suspect.

But just as we earlier saw the limitations of finance-based investment appraisal techniques, for the same reasons, financial standards on their own will also produce skewed value sets. That this is becoming increasingly recognized is reflected in the fact that new standards bodies such as Total Quality Management (TQM), the EFQM Excellence model, the Supply Chain Council, Six Sigma, and many others are working to define nonfinancial standards. These organizations draw on the work of methodology and certification groups and industry consortia to establish and maintain realistic reference models. The supply chain management business process, for instance, contains many specific measures such as on-time delivery and order fill rate, with clearly defined ratios that can be audited and compared.

Appendix B gives some ideas of how standards can be developed under other perspectives.

For the Architecture and Standards Office to operate effectively in the investment process the enterprise as a whole must establish how value standards would yield benefits. The objective is to gain agreement as to why and how the standards will benefit the enterprise, the level of cost and effort involved in meeting them (including staff from the IT customer community), and a willingness and ability to comply with the guidelines. In other words, there will be a trade-off between achieving these desirable objectives, and the cost of doing so. Achieving this level of agreement in the first instance is the responsibility of the IT Council. It *cannot* be delegated to lower level bodies. Ongoing responsibilities include monitoring the state of the project, the degree of compliance, and determining whether relevant projected benefits are achieved. In the event of a serious disagreement over opposing standards, the IT Council will adjudicate.

➤ Role of the Architecture and Standards Office in the Benefits Realization Process

In the investment appraisal process, the Architecture and Standards Office assesses alternatives and helps the IT Investment Board understand the choices, trade-offs, and implications for the architecture, without the need for the Board to understand all the intricate technology that may be involved in complex proposals. While the Board members should balance the integration requirements against those of the users, all technical choices should link their recommendations to business strategy and business drivers. When assessing investment proposals, therefore, the Investment Board will draw on this office for guidance on the proposal's impact on corporate architecture and standards.

■ THE PROJECT OFFICE

The Project Office professionalizes project leadership for the enterprise. As an organizational structure, it is a competency center that provides project managers to business units as well as being a repository of information on best practices and methodology.

Gartner has identified five key roles for a Project Office, although implementations vary based on business structure, the degree of dysfunction, and the sense of urgency across business divisions that a need exists for a shared solution.

➤ *Standard methodology:* The key to implementation—a consistent set of tools and processes for projects—provides a basis for measuring performance and can act as a communication and training vehicle for developing project skills.

➤ *Resource evaluation:* The initial assessment of resources (i.e., people, money, and time) is critical on several fronts. Based on experience and evidence from previous projects, the Project Office validates business assumptions about project and life-cycle costs. It also serves the Investment Board and IT Council by feeding back information that may alter project priorities, based on resource availability or cross-functional project conflicts.

➤ *Project planning:* The project plan is a cooperative effort coordinated by the Project Office, which—as a best practice—serves as a competency center and as a library for previous project plans.

➤ *Project management:* Consistent practices, frequent review, and a governing responsibility are the baseline roles for management within the Project Office. In most initial implementations, project managers are not staffed directly from the Project Office. However, in some organizations, the Project Office is also the source for project managers, who are deployed as consultants—in effect—for the life of the project.

➤ *Project review and analysis:* Enterprises need to know if project goals are achieved on time, on budget, and as designed. The review and analysis phase is a loop back to the resource evaluation role.

Thus, a Project Office can be classed as a shared competency designed to integrate project management skills within an enterprise. In the IT investment appraisal and benefits realization process, the office can play a key role in identifying initial project risk and in instilling best practice techniques in terms of project management and benefits realization. Given appropriate governance, it can improve communication, establish an enterprise standard for project management, and help reduce the effect of failed development projects—and facilitate organizational learning from such failed projects.

➤ **Summary**

These four roles are linked in that the documentation and management of projects lead to better evaluation techniques and a firmer basis for assessing the capability of the organization to achieve business value from its investments.

Gartner best practices emphasize appropriate ownership of IS, the productive interaction of business and IS, and a strong focus on managing the costs and benefits of IT investments. While IT can manage those costs under its control, management of business benefits is primarily a business responsibility. This calls for a clear statement of who is responsible for what at each stage of development, implementation, and use.

Programs should be in place that ensure the interaction and transfer of business and IS skills to both IS and business managers. Disciplined project management and monitoring are essential, as is the willingness to learn from mistakes. Serious efforts must then be made to ensure that benefits tracking and benefits management programs are in place, and that the appropriate managers have these as part of their articulated accountabilities.

I emphasize again that decisions about critical IT investments are the joint responsibility of business and IT management. Governance structures and processes are an essential part of managing the People dimension. They provide transparent pathways for different levels of involvement, decision making, and the allocation and acceptance of responsibilities. Sound processes provide the mechanisms that enable business and technology executives, managers, and professionals to integrate business and technology planning, to implement and monitor key business and technology initiatives, and to track and learn from their effectiveness.

You have to manage the People factor to achieve business value from your IT investments. It is all too easy to fall into old ways of doing things, avoid responsibility, and for senior management to lose practical interest. By way of contrast, effective governance mechanisms ensure that roles, processes, accountabilities, and metrics are assigned and agreed. Everyone knows what needs to be done, who needs to do it, and how success will be judged. There will be a greater sense of fairness and organizational learning will be greatly enhanced. Implementing—and maintaining—this is not a trivial or temporary exercise. Its success will be crucially dependent on the ongoing support and commitment of the CEO. He or she must sell the vision, whip up enthusiasm, communicate, and evangelize, getting across the key message—effective governance is an absolutely mandatory requirement.

■ SUMMARY AND NEXT STEPS

I began this book by seeking to link the demonstrably poor returns from IT investments with a form of management thinking that is from an earlier time, and which is no longer suitable for present day requirements. I took some time to explain the importance of understanding why this is so. In particular, I emphasized the need to assess investments from a broader range of perspectives than has been done traditionally. This assessment needs to be comprehensive and balanced. I believe the framework outlined in the book addresses this. A second major assertion made has been that, even when the "right" IT investment is made, there is no guarantee that this will result in the anticipated business benefits. Benefits have to be proactively managed and measured from the outset of the evaluation process. The framework provides practical and effective guidelines for achieving this.

The framework is based on the 3 Ps, Pillars, Process, and People. The comprehensiveness is covered by the Five Pillars, the methodology itself in the six steps of the Process, and the structures for managing the People dimension have been allocated to each step in the Process. Embodied in those steps are a number of key requirements, including measurement, accountabilities, IT value project management, and the total cost of owning the assets procured.

However, the framework is no panacea or magic bullet. All too many grandiose claims are made for each new management fad, and few have lived up to expectations. The framework is a practical guide to help you invest wisely in IT, realize the benefits, and then manage them. If it does this for you, it must be regarded as a remarkable success, given the record to date. And it can do it, but it won't come about without a degree of preparation, the willingness of people throughout your organization to change the way they've done things before, and maybe even to cede or share a little bit of authority. This could be a challenge, because almost nobody likes change. But think of the rewards—actually achieving expected benefits from your IT investments!

➤ Implementing the Framework

My recommended first implementation step is a program of education and awareness. You'll find it hard to get beyond first base if the key stakeholders don't understand that there is a problem, why there is a problem, and why they need to adopt such a framework to resolve it. Think back to the case of the ZAPped manufacturer. The ERP system was a good fit for enterprise objectives, it was implemented according to plan. But the benefits did not accrue. I believe (and my view is shared by company management) that had the principles of the framework been understood by the key stakeholders, the result would have been so much better.

Communicate, evangelize, hold workshops and feedback sessions. Above all, get top management support and commitment. To get this, management will have to understand the new thinking as well. Because success of the framework calls for cross-departmental cooperation, such support from the top is vital. You'll find that when the concepts are explained in business terms, and the potential value to the enterprise identified, top management will give their support more easily than you might expect. The problem is they also tend to let such support wither faster than you'd expect, so work at maintaining the commitment.

Setting up the Value Standards and the related metrics will likely be seen as a major and intimidating challenge, the perception being that of overloading the Office of Architecture and Standards. This is a legitimate concern but can be addressed in a number of ways.

In the context of the role-based model, this Office is really the "virtual vehicle" for fulfilling the role and does not necessarily require full-time staffing and dedicated resources. There would be a significant up-front effort required in defining an initial set of standards, and in this the Office might need some external assistance. This initial work would focus on defining the first set of standards. Thereafter, the work would involve revising the standards in line with changing business and technology developments. This should not be too labor intensive and could piggyback to some extent on any other IT strategic planning activity. Make sure that the Office is not dominated by "techies." The skills profile would want to be broadened to incorporate business, finance, and HR personnel to fulfill the broader requirements identified in Chapter 3. Again, the role-based approach is a very good fit in this context because these skills may be borrowed from the relevant functional areas as distinct from being dedicated full time to this Office. Such standards should be in place even if you are not implementing the framework. These standards are required for effective business operations. Finally, it is hugely helpful if they are based on and integrated with existing measurement processes, especially those based on Activity-Based Costing (ABC).

Unless yours is a very large organization, I recommend that the various "People" groups (e.g., IT Investment Board) be set up on a "virtual" basis initially. Trying to get commitment to new full-time positions is always a challenge. If possible select a small, relatively self-contained project as the first one. Try for the quick win and ensure that recognition is given for success when merited. Quite apart from the realization of benefits, you'll also see some added value when you implement the framework. You'll find that internal barriers begin to break down, that there will be a common language that enables technical and business staff to interact more effectively, there will be a proactive rather than reactive attitude, there will be a greater perception of fairness in that everyone knows the basis for approving resources for IT investments, and the experience gained should be reflected in enhanced corporate knowledge. There will be a greater feeling of confidence in relation to IT investment decisions. Bear in mind, this does not call for a major bureaucratic structure. In fact, when the process is in place, the net effect will be less use of time, because people know what they have to do, the success factors are clear, resulting in fewer ad hoc meetings and less crisis management.

Lead your organization into a new way of capitalizing on IT, and then make it part of the ongoing business management process. The potential rewards are great, and the need is even greater. Hopefully this book will act as a spur and a support for your efforts.

Appendix A

Sample Value Standards

■ STRATEGIC ALIGNMENT

Mergers/acquisitions/alliances/divestitures

Corporate or brand image/public perception

Improve share price

Suppliers moving up (becoming competitors—possibility of preemptive lockout)

Better alignment with peaks and troughs

Staff empowerment/reduced need for supervision

Improve self-image of staff (staff operating in high-tech environment)

Better corporate image

Improve competitive rankings

Support new geographical markets

Improve visibility of value chains

Support introduction of new products

Formalize innovation

Capture tacit knowledge

Improve knowledge transfer

Improve customer retention

Improve existing customer profitability

Facilitate new customer acquisition

Enhance customer knowledge

Enhance employee knowledge

Enhance reuse capabilities

Facilitate better balance between products and services

Enable more flexible product and service pricing

Support establishment of customer communities

Enable the development of new products and IP

Shorten the development cycle of new products

Reduce dependence on individual suppliers or customers

Enhance linkages with customers and/or suppliers

Support new distribution channels (e-business, agents, direct sale)

Improve efficiency through outsourcing (IT, distribution, contact center)

Reduce dependence on individual employees

Improve compliance and reporting

Capacity to adapt to regulatory requirements

Increase market share

Improve understanding of competitive landscape

Improve security and confidentiality

Support for continuous improvement

Raise skills level of the workforce

Improve levels of employee retention

Improve environmental controls

Flatten management hierarchy

More flexible reward systems

Adopt a more external focus

■ PAYBACK

➤ Direct Cost Savings

Reduce staff
Reduce overtime
Reduce level of h/w investment
Reduce h/w or s/w maintenance
Reduce use of consumables (e.g., stationery)
Reduce inventories
Reduce stock write-offs (obsolescence, scrap, damage, etc.)
Reduce travel costs (video-conferencing, e-mail, multimedia products)
Reduce communications costs (use of IP)
Better purchase prices due to improved supplier management
Improved stock security (e.g., better audit features)
Improved cashflow
Reduce production, sales or stock storage space
Less need for specialized (more expensive) staff
Taxation implications

➤ Quality

Reduce backorders
Fewer recalls/returns
Fewer customer complaints
Better response from customer surveys
Fewer mistakes in invoicing/delivery, etc.
Reduce order/delivery time span
Less reworking

➤ Productivity

Higher sales per employee

More throughput per employee

Fewer phone calls, memoranda, etc.

Less searching for information

Fewer queries (employees handle their own problems better)

Better alignment with peaks and troughs

Revenue earnings

Reduce or eliminate production or delivery bottlenecks

Reduce or eliminate nonvalue adding tasks

Reduce order turnaround time

Reduce audit costs due to better information and/or documentation

Faster access to information

Better online help to reduce support costs

Reduce rekeying of data

Reduce manual aggregating of data

Reduce idle time

More focused plant maintenance

Improve asset utilization

➤ Employee Performance

Better quality of information (less wasted time)

Reduce frustration

Empowerment/reduced need for supervision

Fewer occasions for mistakes

Easier to recover from mistakes

Reduce need for training (system more intuitive or provides enhanced functionality)

Easier to recruit staff (system environment in wide usage)

More flexible working conditions

Improve self-image (staff applying high-tech)

Safer environment

Reduce absenteeism

➤ **Management Performance**

Better information

Faster information

Improve decision support capability

Reduce number of meetings due to better information

■ ARCHITECTURE

Consistency with existing/planned architecture

Terms for preemptive use of technology (workflow, EDI, online marketing, expert systems, electronic cash)

Support increased volumes

Levels of security and DRP

Support for IT asset management

Integration standards (operating system, middleware, networks, database, data)

Legacy system migration

Capacity to link with third party products (spreadsheets, etc.)

Support new and/or additional applications (hardware, data, interfaces)

Support new lines of business

Degree of flexibility required

Supports mergers/acquisitions/alliances

Enables rapid deployment of new applications

Centralization/decentralization

Integrate with outsourced processes

Easier to recruit staff (system environment in wide usage)

Improve reuse of software

Portability

Lower maintenance costs

■ BUSINESS PROCESS IMPACT

More flexible work practices

Reduce/eliminate nonvalue adding activities (unnecessary checks)

Facilitate a process approach

Support multiproduct delivery

Integrate with trading partner processes

Reduce design and development time

Flexibility to reflect new business requirements

Reduce data duplication

Leverage existing data

Support economies of scale

Minimize adaptation costs

Learn from mistakes

Support parallel processing

■ RISK

Scale of project

Definitional uncertainty

Supplier technical or financial uncertainty

Hardware new/untried

Hardware old/outdated

Software new/untried

Software old/outdated

Organizational preparedness

Time frame—the longer the greater the risk

Number of departments involved

Top management awareness/involvement

In-house skills

Vendor technical strength

Vendor financial strength

Vendor vision

Appendix B

Sample Value Standards Scoring Metrics

■ BUSINESS PROCESS IMPACT

Given the nature of this pillar, of necessity, the respective measurement scales are more qualitative than for some of the other pillars.

Standard	Scoring Measurement Scale (0–5)
1. Level of business conducted through nontraditional channels.	This standard might apply in the case of a business seeking to implement a new channel strategy. The 0–5 measurement scale would be equated to a target dollar amount or orders (sales and/or purchase) conducted through new channels facilitated by the new investment. Cannibalization of existing channels would have to be factored in.

(continued)

Standard	Scoring Measurement Scale (0–5)
2. Ability of technology to cope with changing business processes.	Dependent on the specific nature of an investment. Would be measured using a scale similar to the following: 0—Impedes business process change. 1—Provides passive process change support (e.g., provides core transaction support but requires human SOPs for process definition). 2—Provides basic process change support (e.g., new forms and reports may be developed but underlying process model is passive at best). 3—Allows for configuration of some key process areas. 4—Allows for configuration of all key process areas. 5—Provides totally configurable business process support.
3. Support for predefined best-in-class business processes.	The 0–5 measurement scale in this case would be dependent on the proportion of an organizations key business processes for which a best-in-class model is supported: 0—0% 3—60% 1—20% 4—80% 2—40% 5—100%
4. Ability of technology to measure process performance.	The 0–5 measurement scale in this case would be dependent on the proportion of an organization's key business processes for which automated measurement of areas such as effectiveness, efficiency, and flexibility could be achieved. 0—0% 3—60% 1—20% 4—80% 2—40% 5—100%
5. Ability of technology to support new organizational structures.	Particularly relevant in circumstances where an organization is considering downsizing or right-sizing. 0—Technology best suited to specific organizational model. 1— 2— 3— 4— 5—Technology proven to work for multiple organizational models.

Standard	Scoring Measurement Scale (0–5)
	Scale levels 1–4 inclusive dependent on organizations objectives (e.g., centralized structure, decentralized structure, hybrid structure, etc.).
6. Ability of technology to be supported by internal expertise	If the type of technology under consideration can be supported by internal expertise then business process improvement may be achieved more easily than if external expertise is routinely required. 0—Even minor changes require external expertise. 1—Minor changes may be performed by internal personnel (e.g., form and report amendments). 2—Medium level changes may be conducted by internal personnel (e.g., process rerouting or role authorization). 3—Advanced level changes may be conducted by internal personnel (e.g., business rules may be amended). 4—Significant process changes may be enacted by internal personnel (e.g., role redefinition, process dependency modification). 5—New business processes may be fully defined by internal personnel.

■ ARCHITECTURE

Standard	Scoring Measurement Scale (0–5)	
1. Level of compatibility with preferred desktop environment.	0—Not compatible 1— 2—	3— 4— 5—Fully compatible
2. Level of compatibility with preferred server environment.	0—Not compatible 1— 2—	3— 4— 5—Fully compatible
3. Level of compatibility with preferred host environment.	0—Not compatible 1— 2—	3— 4— 5—Fully compatible
4. Level of compatibility with preferred database standard.	0—Not compatible 1— 2—	3— 4— 5—Fully compatible
5. Level of compatibility with preferred development environment.	0—Not compatible 1— 2—	3— 4— 5—Fully compatible
6. Level of compatibility with preferred middleware framework.	0—Not compatible 1— 2—	3— 4— 5—Fully compatible
7. Level of compatibility with preferred networking standard.	0—Not compatible 1— 2—	3— 4— 5—Fully compatible

■ RISK

Standard	Scoring Measurement Scale (0–5)
1. Organizational experience with major IT initiatives.	0—No previous experience 1— 2— 3— 4— 5—Successfully completed many similar initiatives previously
2. Maturity of technological area under consideration.	0—"Bleeding edge" 1— 2— 3— 4— 5—Tried and tested
3. Past experience of organizations from same business sector with this type of technology.	0—No previous experience 1— 2— 3— 4— 5—Many successful installations
4. Project scope.	0—Wide, difficult to clearly define 1— 2— 3— 4— 5—Narrow, well-defined
5. Project duration.	0—Greater than 36 months 1—25–36 months 2—13–24 months 3—7–12 months 4—4–6 months 5—0–3 months

Appendix C

Completed Weightings

Case Study	Strategic Alignment	Business Process Impact	Architecture	Direct Payback	Risk
1. Gung-Ho CEO	5	30	20	40	5
2. Secretive Bank	30	30	10	10	20
3. Silo Myopia	20	30	10	20	20
4. Who Feels the Pain Feels the Gain	10	40	30	10	10
5. The ZAPped Manufacturer	10	30	10	30	20

From the Field—Investment Case Worked Example

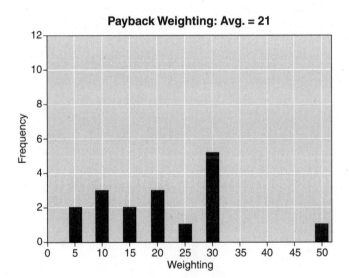

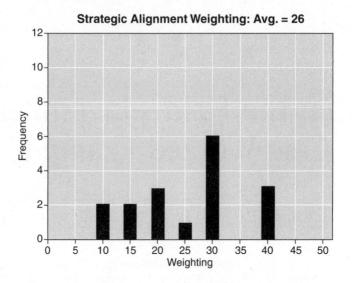

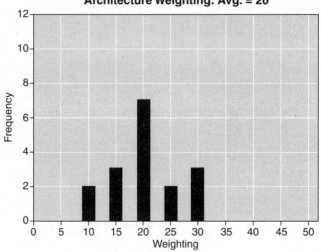

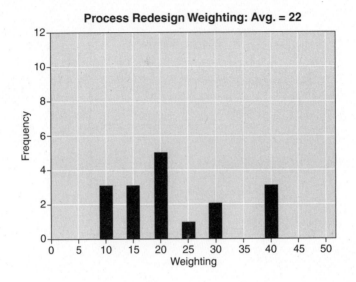

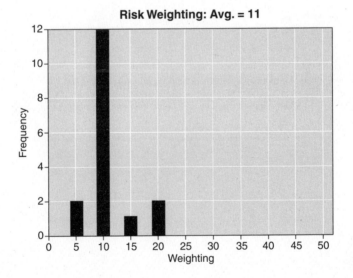

Results Summary

Perspective	Average Weighting
Payback	21
Strategic Alignment	26
Architecture	20
Process Redesign	22
Risk	11

Main Observations

- Weightings exhibiting a wide variance require further discussion to achieve better concensus.

- The averaged results indicate a balanced approach to investment in IT with a slight bias toward achieving strategic alignment even if some risk has to be accepted.

Payback Questions: 1	
Question	*Score*
Will the system support a reduction in inventory levels and obsolesence write-offs? 　　Provided the demand figures are accurate, the regular updating of the Product Profile and subsequently the ABC inventory analysis should result in greater accuracy in scheduling the process. Target savings in inventory levels would be 1 WFC equating to $1.5 million approximately.	10
Will there be a reduction in staff and/or overtime costs? 　　Staff cost savings as per the BPI project for Operations Planning will be underpinned. 　　There is also the possibility of achieving a reduction in overtime costs but this depends on future plans regarding processes on weekend work.	6

Payback Questions: 2	
Question	*Score*
Will there be a reduced level of hardware and software investment and maintenance? 　　No. However, future developments will be much more cost effective.	3
Will there be a reduced level of overhead costs? 　　Increased usage of electronically transmitted data and screen access to information will mean less paperwork and reduced costs in this area. 　　Reduced overhead costs associated with staff cost savings as per the BPI project will be underpinned.	3

Other Payback Questions

Question	Score
Will the system reduce the need for specialized staff in the Production Planning Department?	6
Will the system contribute to a reduction in backorders and complaints and the costs of dealing with same?	3
Will the system contribute to a reduction in rework (e.g., retubbing/repacking) and the costs of dealing with same?	3
Will there be fewer phone calls and queries?	8
Will there be increased production efficiency?	3
Will there be a reduction in audit costs?	2
Is there a reduced need for supervision?	5
Will there be a reduced need for training?	2
Will it be less time consuming and hence less expensive to recruit new staff?	3
Will more flexible working conditions apply, thus, achieving savings associated with increased flexibility under this heading?	0

Strategic Alignment Questions: 1

Question	Score
Will it help us to consistently conform to the expectations of our customers? Without doubt this system will contribute to the scheduling of production in the optimum fashion for our customers and help us to consistently meet their order fulfilment expectations.	10
Will it help us build a partnership with our employees and provide opportunities for individual growth, encouraging teamwork, initiative, and entrepreneurial spirit? The introduction of this system will provide employees in the Planning Department with the opportunity to further improve the quality of service which they provide and to develop new skills in both production planning and the exploitation of IT.	6

Strategic Alignment Questions: 2

Question	Score
Will it help us manufacture and distribute quality products in the most cost effective way to make a profit? This system will provide facilities to help us minimize WIP, inventory and production costs and will certainly contribute to our cost effectiveness.	10
Will it help us continuously improve to ensure the long-term future of the plant? This system will provide facilities to measure, analyze, and understand the planning and scheduling processes on an ongoing basis, thus, providing a solid platform for continuous improvement and long-term benefits.	8

Further Strategic Alignment Questions

Question	Score
Will it help us continuously improve to ensure the long-term future of the plant?	8
Will it help us provide the core skills to our customers?	0
Will it help us act in partnership with our community to improve the quality of life?	0
Will it help improve our ability to manage variations between demand and capacity?	8
Will our communications links with customers improve?	8
How does the time frame for system implementation align with the achievement of our business objectives?	9
Will the system facilitate a reduced level of dependence on individual employees, customers, or suppliers?	3
Can it be easily and quickly adapted in the event of change associated with today's business environment?	8

Architecture Questions: 1

Question	Score
Is it consistent with existing and planned architecture? No system yet has been selected. The final system will be compatible with the planned architecture as it will be "open" and easily integrated.	8
Does the planned architecture preemptively address any of our future requirements? The planned architecture is inherently scaleable, thus, facilitating the easy addition of new users, new processes, and increased functionality.	9

Architecture Questions: 2

Question	Score
Is the planned architecture consistent with industry standards? The planned architecture will conform to worldwide industry standards and, because of this, will ensure good availability of skilled IT staff, knowledgeable vendor support, and good availability of off-the-shelf industy-specific software and hardware modules.	8
Is the planned architecture sufficiently flexible in light of the company's business requirements? The planned architecture will provide the flexibility necessary to support either the centralized or decentralized systems options currently under consideration.	9

Further Architecture Questions

Question	Score
Does the planned architecture have the capacity to link with third-party products?	9
Does the planned architecture have the capacity to support new and/or additional applications?	6
Does the planned architecture have the capacity to cater for new lines of business?	9
Does the planned architecture have the capacity to link with third-party products?	9
Is the planned architecture capable of supporting outsourcing?	8

Business Process Redesign Questions: 1

Question	Score

Could it provide greater flexibility in work practices?
      Only in so far as improved information on process
      and people facilitates this.
	3

Will it reduce/eliminate nonvalue adding activities
(unnecessary checks)?
      Yes. Current manual analysis of large printed reports
      and extensive spreadsheet usage will be largely
      eliminated resulting in increased opportunity for
      information analysis and obviating the need for
      nonvalue adding data gathering and rekeying.
	10

Business Process Redesign Questions: 2

Question	Score

Can existing data be leveraged to provide re-engineering
opportunities which have, up to now, remained hidden?
      Much of the business process improvement work
      performed by the NIMT in both Sarasota and
      Rochester was based on the development of bus-
      iness process databases. In essence these process
      databases brought together data from various
      systems used by various departments (e.g., sales,
      production planning, manufacturing, engineering,
      etc.). Using this technique, business processes
      which spanned multiple departments became
      "visible," measureable, and ultimately improveable.
      The introduction of the scheduling system on the
      planned architecture could be a first step in this
      direction for Waterford.
	7

Can it be easily amended to reflect new requirements?
      Yes. The selected system will be easily amended to
      reflect new production process, scheduling, reporting,
      and analysis requirements.
	10

Further BPR/BPI Questions

Question	Score
Does it facilitate a process approach to business rather than reinforcing function-based operations? The plant-wide availability of operational and management information from the scheduling system will certainly support the process approach to business while still allowing the Production Planning Department to attain its specific targets.	10
Could it prevent existing practices from becoming too embedded? The system would provide insights into the effectiveness of existing practices more than embedding them in a concealed fashion and would provide powerful flexibility in the development of streamlined ways of implementing business processes.	8

Risk Questions: 1

Question	Score
Does the scale of the project contribute to the risk of failure (0 = Yes, 10 = No)? Ultimately the scale of the project will be quite large if the resultant system is to be deployed in a number of B&L plants. In this context risk of failure would be quite high if a short time frame was envisaged for complete system development and deployment. The strategy of developing as simple a system as possible for the commencement of cast-mould toric production with subsequent phased development of additional features will minimize development risk.	7

Risk Questions: 2

Question	Score
Is the vendor reliable in terms of technical capability, financial strength? The selected vendor will be reliable. However, the availability of technical resources within the *target time frame* represents a substantial risk. The availability of Speedware resources represents an even bigger risk as it is virtually certain that the resources required to develop on this platform will not be available.	5
Are the hardware or software platforms stable and current? The software and hardware that will be used are new to the company but standard in the industry. From a technological perspective their reliability is not in question but the company faces a learning curve in their exploitation.	6

Further Risk Questions

Question	Score
Is the organization prepared for the introduction of the system? The IM&T department will certainly need training and development to manage the technical dimension of the project. Outside resources will most likely be used to augment internal IM&T resources. Top management support for the system implementation will be vital and forthcoming. Therefore, under this heading, there is some risk but it is manageable.	8
Is there a risk associated with the number of departments spanned by the project? Quite a large number of departments are involved in one form or another with this project, including the following—Production Planning, IM&T, Business Planning, Production, Customer Service, QA. The major stakeholders are Production Planning and IM&T and, while the large number of departments involved does pose some risk, it is not hugely significant due to the dominance of just two major departments.	8

Weighting Guidelines

- Award questions a weighting in the range 1 to 10.
    Note: A weighting of 0 implies that a question is irrelevant.

- Initially award the most important question a rating
  of 10 and weight other questions relative to this.

- When the organization becomes comfortable with
  the methodology then weightings can be determined
  using organizationwide standards.

Assign Weights to the Strategic Alignment Questions
Shown Below (Marks out of 10)

Question	Weight
Will it help us to consistently conform to the expectations of our customers?	
Will it help us build a partnership with our employees and provide opportunities for individual growth, encouraging teamwork, initiative, and entrepreneurial spirit?	
Will it help us continuously improve to ensure the long-term future of the plant?	
Will it help us provide core skills to our customers?	
Will it help us act in partnership with our community to improve the quality of life?	
Will it help improve our ability to manage variations between demand and capacity?	
Will our communications links with customers improve?	
How does the time frame for system implementation align with the achievement of our business objectives?	
Will the system facilitate a reduced level of dependence on individual employees, customers, or suppliers?	
Can it be easily and quickly adapted in the event of change associated with today's business environment?	

Assign Weights to Payback Questions Shown Below (Marks out of 10)

Question	Weight
Will the system support a reduction in inventory levels and obsolesence write-offs?	
Will there be a reduction in staff and/or overtime costs?	
Will the system reduce the need for specialized staff in the Production Planning Department?	
Will the system contribute to a reduction in backorders and complaints and the costs of dealing with same?	
Will the system contribute to a reduction in rework (e.g., retubbing/repacking) and the costs of dealing with same?	
Will there be fewer phone calls and queries?	
Will there be increased production efficiency?	
Will there be reduction in audit costs?	
Will there be a reduced need for supervision?	
Will there be a reduced need for training?	
Will it be less time consuming and hence less expensive to recruit new staff?	

Weighting of Other Questions

- Apply similar approach to other perspectives:
  - Architecture.
  - Business Process Redesign.
  - Risk (note that even though risk *scores* are inverted, risk *weights* are awarded in the usual manner, i.e., questions relating to high risks are heavily weighted).

Calculate Score by Perspective

• Compute weighted average by perspective as follows:

Question	Weight	Score	Value
Question 1	10	7	70
Question 2	5	6	30
Question 3	7	9	63
Question 4	3	4	12
Total			175

• Total Potential Score = (10+5+7+3)×10 = 250
• Weighted Average Score = 175/250 = 0.7 = 70%

Apply Weightings by Perspective to Weighted Averages

Perspective	Average Weighting	Score*	Value
Payback	21	70%	15%
Strategic alignment	26	80%	21%
Architecture	20	90%	18%
Process redesign	22	65%	14%
Risk	11	50%	6%
Total			74%

* Scores estimated for presentation purposes.

Interpretation of Overall Scores

Overall Score Range	Interpretation
0%–25%	Likely to be a very poor investment.
26%–50%	Has some potential but will likely require significant modification before approval.
51%–75%	Likely to be a good investment but may need some fine-tuning.
76%–100%	Almost certainly a solid investment.

Final Summary

- The main benefit of the methodology described is that it provides companies with a tool to support *balanced* IT investment appraisal.

- The methodology should become more organization-specific with usage.

- The methodology provides a solid linkage between business and IT strategies.

Appendix

Quantifying
End-User Benefits

Quantifying the benefits of end-user computing is particularly challenging. This is largely due to the difficulty in determining the *productivity* of white-collar workers. Though not easy, we can improve enormously from what is commonly done today (i.e., virtually no attempt at quantification). It all depends on how you go about it, especially the interviewing technique. Traditional interviewing techniques have been shown to be inadequate in identifying, and more particularly in quantifying, savings and other gains from end-users, particularly from managers, given the nature of their work. The following seven-stage approach has proved effective in identifying and quantifying benefits that may otherwise have not been achieved.

■ PRELIMINARY INFORMATION

Gather as much preliminary information as possible relating to the user's job and key performance indicators. These should ideally be derived from a number of sources, not just the individual. The sources could include the corporate strategic plan (assuming there is one), company annual reports, and departmental or management review meetings.

▪ OPENING THE MEETING

A heavily structured, questionnaire-style interview is unlikely to be fully effective. Better results are achieved when the effort is directed toward determining what the interviewee does, and what he perceives as the factors that determine success for him personally. Experience shows that this will not come easily, as the interviewee will frequently provide "company line" or self-serving answers, or those that he feels the interviewer wants to hear. Therefore, it is important initially that the interviewer expresses interest in the job in the broadest sense, gives the interviewee adequate opportunity to discuss the job/project, and give his views freely.

Asking whether his job or department is afforded due recognition, or how he feels the department's performance could be improved can be fertile sources of information, as can a discussion on his likely career path. The objective is to gain an enhanced appreciation for what he believes his objectives to be, and to be in a position to evaluate whether these are in accordance with corporate objectives as determined earlier. Given the variety of jobs and the range of personality types, a structured questionnaire is unlikely to provide the requisite scope and flexibility. This is not to say that a certain structure should not underlie all interviews. Such a structure is necessary, but should be used more as preparation for the interview than in the form of a questionnaire.

▪ RESOLUTION OF INCONSISTENCIES

Where an answer has been given that appears at variance with information received earlier (either as part of the preliminary investigation, or as part of the interview), a direct challenge is inappropriate. A subsequent gradual raising of the same point via another route is more effective. An example might be where both organizational objectives and the interviewee define "100 percent fulfillment of customer orders" as the critical success factor. However, the interviewer may have the perception that low inventory carrying costs may be what really matters. A more realistic response might then be obtained by redirecting the conversation to, for instance, the pressures that apply in performing his tasks efficiently. A short discussion of this could be followed by a statement like "it must be very important, and very difficult, to keep down inventory carrying costs when you are providing such a high level of service." Given plenty of time and encouragement, he will probably reveal his real motivational factors more accurately.

■ QUANTIFYING THE BENEFITS

Quantifying benefits in the realm of end-user computing, particularly when it relates to managers, is recognized as an unpromising task, with benefits generally being classified as the intangible variety. Yet, the scale of investment in these areas calls for the maximum endeavor to be made in seeking to firm up on the benefits where possible. Direct pressure on the user to quantify benefits usually gives rise to defensiveness, a lack of frankness, or a retreat into vagueness. One of the most common reactions when asked to specify the benefits of a new system will be "better and faster information," possibly with the rider that it is impossible to quantify the value of such benefits.

Rather than focus on the specific benefits, seek to identify one specific benefit that would have been achieved with the system, with a view to expanding this into identifying the full scope of the benefits. The following simulated dialogue, beginning with a response to the "better and faster information" reply, demonstrates a typical scenario:

INTERVIEWER: "That must be useful. How does it specifically help you in your work?"

Some specifics may be provided, for example, sales quotations can be submitted earlier, and be more effective through the use of better information.

INTERVIEWER: "I can see why you like the system. I wonder how often does this actually result in additional or better deals?

For instance, can you recollect even one occasion in which the system made a difference, or were there close calls before the system was introduced when it could have made a difference?"

If no instance is provided, it can reasonably be assumed that the system is not providing tangible benefits, unless the extra time the user now has is being availed of by way of additional tasks, or enhanced decision-making capability (see below). The user is in fact more likely to name one or more instances where the system has, or could have, made a difference. Rather than seeking to quantify as this stage, the user should be encouraged to talk more about it, without undue prompting. This could be followed by a comment such as "from what you say, there could have been other examples as well" and, if appropriate, suggest possibilities. In the discourse that inevitably follows, further possibilities may be identified.

Now is the time to attempt quantification of benefits.

INTERVIEWER: "It seems you'll make great use of the system. Looking back, it seems that maybe up to five additional sales may have been made over the last year had you had it at the time. Would you think this is realistic?"

Clearly, this runs the risk of putting words in the user's mouth. The risk must be set against the need for quantification, and if the interviewer has established a reasonable degree of trust, should not present undue distortion.

It is now possible to quantify the profit potential of the additional sales (taking average margin per sale and multiplying it by the number of sales). This can be used for subsequent measurement on how the system actually performed. If the benefits are subsequently not realized, the process should be repeated along the original lines. The objective would not be to apportion blame, rather to learn from the process, and incorporate what was learned into future evaluations and proposals.

■ REFINE QUANTIFICATION

As described earlier, benefits are often presented, especially by managers, as intangibles, frequently along the lines of "faster information." Receiving the information faster does not automatically translate into business benefit. An appropriate response would be "How do you find that useful?" This provides a sharper focus, and frequently, what seems to be a clear-cut benefit turns out to be no benefit at all, once the user has the time to think the process through by responding to the question. In the example quoted, it may turn out that getting the information faster has no practical impact on achieving the user's objectives.

Additional degrees of refinement can be achieved by focusing on the constituent elements of the claimed benefits. For instance, should the user say, "the system saves time" it should be established, using the techniques described above, whose time and how much is saved, and how often. Again, it is essential that this be established without the introduction of a confrontational element.

■ CROSS-VERIFICATION

Continuous cross-verification of the information given during the interview(s) is important, but this should be done tactfully. For instance, if, reverting to the example last described, the user claims the system "saves time" it has been found that, rather than asking "What do you do with the extra time?" a more effective approach was to raise the issue at a later stage, ideally in a different form. This could be presented as "Do you find that the system enables you to do things now that you could not do before?" If the reply is in the negative, it does not necessarily mean he had been wrong in claiming it saved time, or that he is wasting the time saved. A further question subsequently along the lines of "Have you found in any way that the system gives you more time to actually do the job better?" can reveal the true benefits. In the case of an affirmative answer, a follow-up question such as "That's good. Do you find yourself doing things now that you did not do before?" may prove useful. This may reveal definite benefits, or alternatively, that the supposed enhanced quality is largely in the user's mind. The principle is one of self-checking, without making it appear to be self-checking.

This seven-point interviewing technique should not be regarded as an end in itself, rather as an added resource for determining system benefits. Results should be validated against other yardsticks, which will vary considerably between organizations.

The approach does have its limitations. It is dependent to a considerable degree on the knowledge and judgment of the users, the skills of the interviewer, and on the personality interplay between the interviewer and the user. Furthermore, it runs the risk of "leading" the interviewee. However, given the extent of the difficulties experienced in quantifying end-user benefits, less than scientifically rigorous methods may have to be tolerated, especially in the light of the frequently amorphous and intangible nature of those benefits.

Clearly, the technique is not one that can be "learned" as such. It requires practice and experience for each interviewer to fine-tune his techniques, and these will undoubtedly need to be tailored to adapt to different individual and organizational characteristics. Lessons learned from the exercises should contribute to organizational learning, and be incorporated into future appraisals of system proposals. However, the technique can be hugely beneficial in identifying and quantifying benefits that otherwise would have gone untracked. It also strengthens a sense of accountability and adds to the corporate wisdom bank.

Appendix F

Gartner Recommended Approach to Risk Management

■ COLLABORATIVE RISK MANAGEMENT

Because IT-related investment assists business managers in securing the benefits expected from their initiatives, it is critical that executives, including the CIO, collaborate to ensure that the benefits are realized and risks associated with nonachievement are minimized. For the collaboration to work effectively, there must be a risk assessment process in place and clear governance roles.

The governance roles and activities need to be formalized, and cover both demand and supply functions as described and depicted in Figure F.1.

The governance roles envisaged are:

➤ *Demand management,* involving pursuit of a business opportunity from concept to the realization of expected net benefits (i.e., gross benefits minus costs). This is typically the overall responsibility of the business sponsor and is often delegated to line managers.

➤ *Supply management,* as it relates to the acquisition of resources to construct and process the application systems

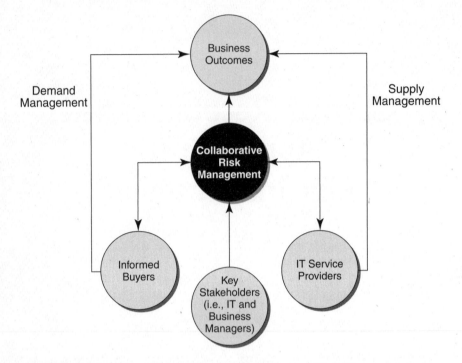

Figure F.1 Interaction of Demand, Supply, and Risk Management

solution on a continuous basis—typically the responsibility of the CIO.

IT infrastructure investment is typically the responsibility of the CIO, from investment proposal to harvesting of expected benefits (i.e., the CIO is involved in both supply and demand management activities).

■ RISK ASSESSMENT PROCESSES

Figure F.2 shows a summary of the processes of a risk assessment lifecycle for collaborative risk management. Successful implementation of risk management processes in the enterprise will be predicated on:

➤ Early identification of risks.

➤ Continuous and objective assessment of the risks.

➤ The executive accepting ultimate ownership of the impact of the risk and activities associated with its minimization.

➤ Line management sharing responsibility for implementing risk minimization strategies.

We will first examine the risk management governance function, then discuss the major steps in the process.

➤ Risk Management Governance Function

The risk management governance function, which might be carried out by the IT Council or board subcommittee or equivalent, must be linked to both demand and supply management activities. It must focus on risk situations that might compromise the realization of expected benefits and develop

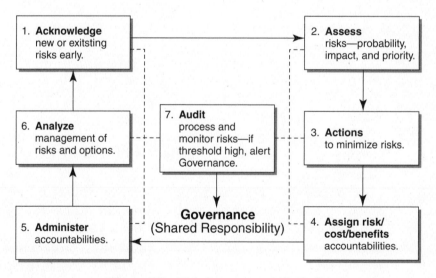

Figure F.2 Risk Assessment Life Cycle

risk minimization strategies (i.e., activities that will negate the risk or reduce its potential impact).

This focus will include:

➤ Existing business systems.
➤ Business systems under development.
➤ Business systems being considered for approval.

The Council should report frequently to the executive or board of the organization and alert them to the major risk events, their consequences, and efforts to eliminate or minimize them.

The Council will be initially responsible for approving:

➤ Processes for risk categorization.
➤ Business impact assessment weightings.
➤ Risk probability determination guidelines.
➤ The probability/impact index threshold (i.e., when the probability is high and potential impact is so serious that it must be reported to the executive).

Risk governance practices have to include guidelines for:

➤ Discontinuing the funding for the program/project if the likelihood of realizing expected benefits is low (e.g., the differentiated services being developed are no longer in demand by the market).
➤ Postponing the program/project until the risks are lower (e.g., legislation is clarified or industrial activity has abated).
➤ Postponing the program/project (e.g., until dependent software has been proven by the vendor or other clients or critical technical resources have been secured).
➤ Reducing the scope and funding of program/project because the expected market or opportunity has shrunk slightly.

➤ Continuing development as per schedule while regularly monitoring risks in the knowledge that the cost of doing nothing is itself too high to contemplate.

Members of the Council will need to have considerable grasp of the impact of implementing aspects of the guidelines above, for example when discontinuing a program/project and having to determine the breakage costs. The Council needs to be asking questions such as:

➤ Have the risks been objectively assessed?
➤ Are the risks overstated?
➤ Has management tried to implement all risk minimization options?
➤ Who will be adversely impacted if the program/project has to be cancelled or postponed?

It is typically in the audit process—not necessarily the function—that the above questions are considered and that escalates the matter to the Council for deliberation and action.

Membership on the Council should include those who have a broad understanding of the ramifications of the risk event being considered and can make an informed contribution to the assessment of the options. This means that it should be restricted to senior managers, including the business sponsor, CIO, program/project manager and other stakeholders. Much organizational learning takes place at Council meetings when all aspects of the risk event are canvassed, business impact assessed, scenarios presented and a course of action determined.

In large organizations, the Council might delegate the role of administering risk management processes to a subcommittee comprised, for instance, of representatives from the IT function and business units. The subcommittee should ideally conduct workshops to air and assess the risks and present options to the Council.

➤ Probability Index

The convenor or facilitator of the workshop must ensure that there is a shared understanding of the issues surrounding the risk event and get consensus on the probability of the event occurring. To simplify the assessment when multiple events are involved, participants should assign a score from 1 to 10, where 10 reflects certainty of occurrence. For the purposes of this paper the score is known as the probability index.

Ideally, opinions expressed on the nature of the risk and the probability of the event occurring should never be accepted at face value, but challenged openly before the assessment is made. It is axiomatic that participants contributing to the

Table F.1 Risk Events and Probability

Occurrence Probability		
Low	Medium	High
Application systems recovery process has been proven previously, but not with current release of software.	Software has been proven in one other client that processes 60 percent fewer transactions.	Software is unproven in country.
Staff have been trained and have needed skills but have not integrated so many software products at the same time.	Comparable processes have not been implemented in firm before.	Because of workload, management defines business processes three months after implementation.
Vendor support in city is sound but not proven on current release of software.	Staff have been trained, but have minimal hands-on experience with the software.	Staff in remote locations will not be able to acquire skills needed with existing training program.
	If failure occurs, some customer-facing processes will be inoperable (status quo can be restored quickly).	Failure of software will compromise service delivery to major clients and adversely impact image.
	Vendors have support center 100 miles away and only one specialist on site.	Vendors are unproven and support center is 500 miles away.

Note: Consider using the Gartner scale to determine the probability index (e.g., low occurrence = 1–4, medium occurrence = 5–7, and high = 8–10).

debate will need to be well informed on the probability of the event occurring.

In Table F.1 are descriptions of possible risk (of failure) events that might occur during the systems lifecycle and the circumstances in which failure might occur. Events are classified from low (might happen) to high probability (i.e., that the event will occur). The list of events is indicative and not exhaustive. Editorial license has been used when assessing the probability of occurrence.

➤ **Impact Index**

In addition to probability, the Council will also need to consider the likely business impact of the event (i.e., its potential to compromise final outcomes). Again, informed business judgment in assessing the impact will be required.

Before making the assessment, the Council will need to endorse the criteria for weighting and scoring the impact. Ideally, weighting should be based on the degree to which the risk event will compromise achievement of one or more corporate goals (see below). The score, expressed as the impact index, should be from 1 to 10, where 10 reflects a devastating and widespread impact. Whether the criteria should be based on the premise that all corporate goals are of equal value or that some are more critical to the viability of the organization than others is a judgment the Council must make.

Typical corporate goals might be:

➤ Achievement of:
  —Planned profit or surplus in public sector.
  —Return on shareholders' funds or equivalent.
➤ Minimization of working capital required.
➤ Provision of services as required by statute and consistent with occupational health and safety parameters.
➤ Maintain a safe workplace with no major accidents.
➤ Compliance with statutory reporting obligations and without audit qualification.

➤ Probability/Impact Index

To give the executive an order of magnitude of the risks and their potential impact, a combined probability impact index should be developed. This might vary from a simple addition of the two indices to the application of weighting to one of them. A simplistic example of how the index might be determined is set out in Table F.2.

The threshold for reporting risk events with an abnormally high index will also need to be agreed to by the Council. The premise used in the example below is that the executive should be engaged when the aggregate index is greater than 10 out of a possible score of 20. Before engaging the executive, the Council

		Table F.2 Probability Impact Index		
Risk Event	Probability Index	Consequential Business Impact	Impact Index	Probability/ Impact Index
Three-month implementation schedule delay because of lack of skilled resources.	6	Delay realization of benefits.	6	12/20
Implementation cost overruns.	6	Turn sound investment proposition into a marginal one.	7	13/20
Competitors erecting a barrier to entry into expected market.	8	Unable to achieve expected volume revenue increase.	8	16/20
Pending industrial activity in firm.	5	Hinder ability to get new products and services to market.	6	11/20
Adverse changes in industry demand for products and services.	4	Potential revenue increase is harder to realize.	5	9/20

should develop risk minimization strategies and present them when providing details of the risk event and its impact.

When developing risk minimization strategies, special emphasis needs to be given to matters outside the control of the organization (e.g., impact of pending legislation). It is often executives who first become aware of these matters and alert line management of their impact.

It is axiomatic that risk events must be continually monitored in case the probability of the event occurring increases suddenly and without warning.

■ PREDICTABILITY AND COMPLEXITY OF RISKS

It is self-evident that the more predictable the business outcome, the lower its risk and its degree of complexity (i.e., because the expected result is clear and the process is easy to administer). Conversely, the more complex the process and the unpredictability of the outcome, the higher the risk and the

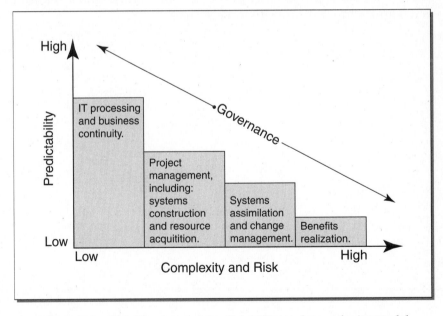

Figure F.3   Risk Managment Predictability and Complexity Model

need to identify it early in the system's lifecycle to forestall an increase in problems. Figure F.3 depicts the relationship between predictability and risks.

In practice CIOs tend to concentrate on activities or situations they understand and over which they have a high degree of control. These activities tend to be on the left side in Figure F.3 and are usually part of the supply management role.

The more abstract areas, such as benefits realization, on the right in Figure F.3, are typically less developed and not well understood. They are also usually an aspect of the demand management role and difficult to implement because they are not everyday activities and often lack empirical data to measure.

■ SUMMARY

If risk management processes and guidelines have been developed in a collaborative fashion, follow sound principles and put into practice, the output should get unqualified acceptance at the executive level. The approach outlined in this appendix is designed to facilitate this acceptance.

Appendix C

Analytical Hierarchy Process/Analysis

Given that dozens of vendors sell nearly any technology, focusing an evaluation by identifying requirements and strong preferences can lead to an overlong list of vendors and products for consideration. Ideally, this list should have no more than five or six candidates. However, being too stringent on functionality requirements can eliminate what could have been the best "overall" solution.

All too often, we see mandatory criteria that are so stringent that no vendor can satisfy them. Thus, we recommend that IS organizations begin with truly mandatory requirements. For example, "Must run on Windows with IBM's DB2 databases as well as in a Unix environment using Oracle databases," might be mandatory while "Support for IBM's OS/2 and other types of databases" might be a "nice-to-have," but not mandatory, criterion. If, after applying the truly mandatory criteria in an analytical hierarchy process (AHP) analysis, more than nine vendors remain, the strongest preferences should probably be applied to shorten the list of candidates to a more manageable number. Conversely, if only one or two remain, the list of mandatory requirements should be scrutinized to ensure its appropriateness.

The AHP extends the traditional evaluation models to achieve:

➤ Homogeneous clustering of variables for meaningful comparisons.

➤ The ability to conduct dynamic sensitivity analysis or "what if" scenarios.

➤ The ability to check the logical consistency of the decision model that the enterprise is using.

Applying this structure to evaluate vendors ensures that the investments of time and money to gather information are not wasted as a consequence of a logically inconsistent structure behind the decision, or because the sensitivity of the conclusion could not be examined adequately.

Hierarchical decomposition, similar to that used in the AHP, is a proven, effective means to deal with complex information. It has been proposed and refined within academic circles and leading-edge businesses for more than 10 years, and is now becoming a mainstream business solution for vendor and product evaluation.

Many times no formalized evaluation process like the AHP is used. Some reasons for not formalizing evaluation are:

➤ Economic consequences of a suboptimal decision are too low to justify the investment in the time required to complete a formalized approach.

➤ Number of choices or criteria being examined is too long to warrant the use of a formalized approach.

➤ Lack of IS organization skills, committed resources, or both.

➤ For reasons of political or technical bias, senior managers do not support the use of a formalized approach.

➤ Decision makers are unwilling to commit to a formalized approach due to cultural or organizational issues or both.

The AHP consists of three steps:

1. Developing the hierarchy of attributes germane to the selection of the vendor.

2. Identifying the relative importance of the attributes.

3. Scoring the alternatives' relative performance on each element of the hierarchy.

In a hierarchical decomposition, the enterprise decomposes the goal of choosing the best IT solution into its constituent parts, progressing from the general to the specific. For instance, when the "goal" is purchasing an application development tool, the vendor offerings should be evaluated based on five major criteria (see Figure G.1):

1. *Product Functionality.* The first major criterion comprises the feature functions necessary to provide a comprehensive solution for developing enterprise applications in a distributed environment. Functionality, in turn, can be divided into four core components:

   Development procedural capabilities.

   Development technology.

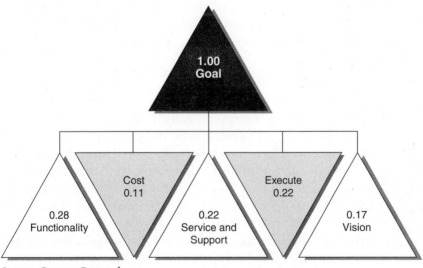

Source: Gartner Research.

Figure G.1 Overall Criteria for AHP

Target platform.

Application platform.

2. *Vendor's ability to execute.* This major criterion considers two factors:

Financial execution capabilities. The technical execution segment explores metrics that reveal the relative quality of the personnel within key departments of the vendor and its ability to meet industry milestones. For instance, it would explore the issue of whether the vendor can fulfill the vision set out by its management.

Technical execution capabilities. The financial execution segment investigates the financial wherewithal of the vendor relative to its peers. Metrics might include: investments in research and development and in sales and marketing; growth in revenue, net margins and employees; and return on assets, equity and investments.

3. *Vendor services and support.* This criterion explores the quality, availability and reliability of the value-added services offered by the product vendor and its third-party alternatives. Areas for investigation include: installation, training and education, consulting, maintenance and the help desk.

4. *Vendor vision.* This criterion examines the vendor's understanding of new and emerging technologies' market impact and how they will be incorporated into the vendor's product and service offerings. It explores the vendors' perspectives on what factors will shape how they will evolve or enhance their technology, product functionality, service and support capabilities and sales and marketing channels. Articulation of a clear and comprehensive strategy in each of these categories is only the beginning; quality execution against established milestones will demonstrate sincerity of stated vision.

5. *Product and services costs.* This criterion evaluates the relative cost of the technology. Cost is important because regardless of the functional fit, service and support, or technical architecture, if the cost of a given application is not within the reach of a given organization, then the other criteria are relatively inconsequential.

The first criterion underneath cost is the initial cost, which evaluates the initial cost of the application. Initial cost examines the total cost of the initial implementation of the model, including not only system license fees, but initial training, installation and consulting fees associated with the installation of the product. The second component of cost is ongoing cost. This component explores the total costs associated with such things as training, maintenance and consulting to support development efforts throughout the tool's lifecycle.

Each parent criterion is broken down into increasing levels of component detail, or "child" criteria.

The relative importance of the criteria resides in the assignment of a weight to each selected criterion. This weight can be either global or local. These weights may be adjusted to see the impact on the final decision. The local weight shows the relative importance of the criterion within its immediate tier. The sum of the weights of all the child criteria beneath a given parent must equal one. For example, using the criteria shown in Figure G.2 as a hypothetical case, assuming Functionality has a weight of 0.28 (i.e., it constitutes 28 percent of the total decision) then, if Development Process—a criterion under Functionality—is 25 percent of the Functionality evaluation (local weight), it is 7 percent (28×0.25) of the overall decision (global weight).

Once the criteria are weighted, the evaluation is ready to examine vendors/tools against these criteria. As vendor information is gathered, the data points are input into the model. The scoring is relative, not absolute (i.e., vendors are scored relative to one another). Next, relative scores are computed for each of the vendors and the scores are synthesized through the

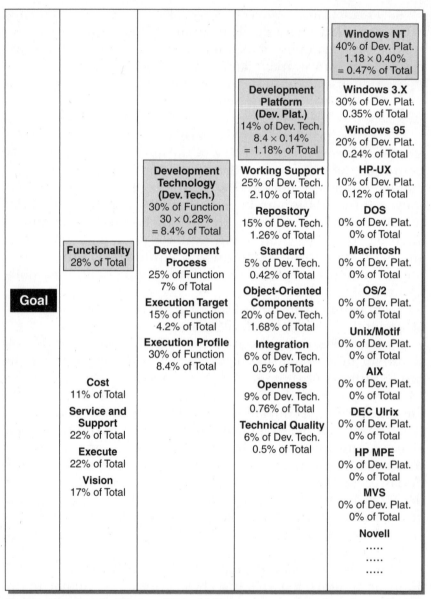

Note: In this example, Windows NT is, for illustrative purposes, the primary development platform.

Source: Gartner Research.

Figure G.2 Calculations for AHP

model. This process yields a composite score for each vendor at every tier of the model, as well as an overall score.

■ AHP: DETAILED EXAMPLE (FUNCTIONALITY EXPANDED)

Figure G.2 examines a detailed example of using the AHP process to evaluate vendors. In this particular case, we look at the goal of selecting the best enterprise application development tool kit. At the highest level the criteria include functionality, cost, service and support, and the ability to execute and vision. For our analysis, we drill down in the area of functionality. Within functionality we examine the development technology of the tool. Specifically in the area of development technology, we investigate the development platform supported by the various application development tool vendors.

Clearly, there are multiple potential development platforms, including DOS, Windows 3.X, Windows 95, Windows NT, OS/2, HP-UX, Unix Motif, AIX, and MVS. For our example, we consider a subset of platforms. Figure G.3 lists mandatory requirements (i.e., those platforms currently supported within the organization and planned for the upcoming project) and future requirements (i.e., those platforms not supported, but planned for the future). The list of mandatory platforms include Windows NT on the server side and Windows 3.X on the client side. The future platforms include HP-UX on the server and Windows 95 on the client.

With these requirements in mind, we see that Vendor D is discarded from the initial list, since the vendor does not support Windows NT (a mandatory requirement). Next we turn to vendors A, B and C, all of which meet the mandatory requirements. To compare these vendors, we look at the future requirements. There the vendors distinguish themselves as well. Vendor A supports Windows 95, and has plans to support HP-UX in the next 12 months; Vendor B supports Windows 95 and HP-UX; and Vendor C supports Windows 95 and has support for HP-UX via customization. As a result, Vendor B receives the highest score for this particular criterion.

Development Platforms (Mandatory Platforms)	Vendor A	Vendor B	Vendor C	Vendor D*
Windows NT	I	I	I	not now >future
Windows 3.x	I	I	I	I
Client Organization Future Support				
HP-UX	future	I	custom (now)	I
Windows 95	I	I	I	I
Development Platforms Supported: Scores	5	9	7	N/A

*Vendor D: eliminated at beginning for not meeting one of the main key criteria.

Figure G.3   Scores after Running AHP at Development Platform Level

To perform a complete analysis, the exercise would be repeated for each of the lowest-level criteria in the model and the scores compiled.

Once weights are assigned to each individual criterion, the AHP is ready to accept the values that will generate the comparisons of the vendors and tools. In considering development platform:

1. Vendors are assigned values from one to nine for each of the child criteria within the development platform.

2. These values are fed into the AHP model that in turn uses pair-wise comparison with cardinal consistency to evaluate the relative importance of the criteria to one another.

3. Specific scores relative to development platform for each vendor come as a result of complex mathematics beneath the model. (*Note:* This assumes that values are entered for every criterion at the development platform level, including Repository, Workgroup Support, and Technology Quality.)

4. By averaging the scores, the model produces final scores for each vendor being compared at that level.

5. The process (steps 1–4 above) is repeated at each level, traversing the tree bottom-up until the goal is reached. (*Note:* The mathematical theory behind the model provides a method for evaluating the impact of one level on an adjacent upper level from the composition of the relative contributions—priority weights—of the elements in that level with respect to each element of the adjacent level—i.e., elements from development platform and from repository. This composition can be then extended upwards through the hierarchy.)

Appendix H

Probability Analysis (Monte Carlo Simulation)

Sensitivity Analysis represents an improvement on a single range of forecast values, but does not address the issue of the degree of certainty with which the various forecasts can be made.

Representing this probability distribution in terms of NPV IRR and Payback Period would be helpful in assessing the likely viability of the project. The Monte Carlo Simulation, developed by Hertz in the 1960s, is a commonly used technique for this purpose. This performs complex, repetitive calculations, hundreds or even thousands of times, which taken together provide a risk profile of the proposed investment. The term Monte Carlo Simulation derives from the element of chance which forms the basis for the exercise. Any project evaluation involves forecasting values based on various assumptions. Certain assumptions may be made with a reasonable degree of certainty, while others may be subject to a wide range of possible outcomes. The purpose of simulation is to try to reproduce the randomness inherent in this concept, thus giving a "most likely picture" to emerge in a real-life situation.

This is achieved by having the system generate random values for selected components. Although random, these values reflect weightings specified by the user. This is important, because while in a real-life situation various unpredictable outcomes may occur, some possible outcomes are clearly more likely to occur than others.

After the simulation has been run, it is possible to make judgments such as "there is a 90 percent chance that the Internal Rate of Return (IRR) will be above 15 percent, and a less than 1 percent chance that it will be below 5 percent." Used in conjunction with the "what-if" facilities, it provides a useful additional tool for evaluating the risk factor involved.

The simulation generates random numbers within the probability ranges defined. It then recalculates the model repeatedly, each time arriving at a different possible outcome (often defined in terms of NPV, IRR, or Payback Period).

To revert to the previous example, for every 10 random numbers generated, the system will generate 6 for the range 10/12,000, 3 in the range 5/10,000, and 1 in the range 12/15,000. The full model will be recalculated each time. The requirement of randomness is met, while simultaneously the weighting ensures that the requirements of probability are also met. Thus, a large number of recalculations based on this methodology provides the closest approximation to a real-life situation, and will represent the most comprehensive picture of the range of possible outcomes, and their likelihood.

Even though the simulation will be performed repeatedly, the final picture produced will consolidate all of the possible outcomes into a single graphical representation (histogram) which will elucidate the risk profile for the project. Only those elements identified through Sensitivity Analysis as likely to have a significant bearing on the outcome of the project should undergo this simulation.

The Monte Carlo simulation is an advance on basic sensitivity techniques because:

➤ It forces consideration of all the major uncertain variables.

➤ It allows these variables to vary independently.

➤ It forces quantification of the risk and variability of outcomes.

➤ The results indicate how likely the expected, best and worst outcome is likely to be.

It does have a drawback in relation to the difficulty of interpreting the result. For example, is it better to select a project with a high spread of results (high risk) but with a higher expected value, or a low spread of results (low risk) but with a lower expected value?

Appendix *I*

Gartner Approach to Change Management: Strategic Planning Assumption

■ THE NEED FOR CHANGE MANAGEMENT

Change management is not just about charm schools and motivational wall posters. It's primarily about understanding and influencing beliefs and behaviors. Because the response to change is predominantly emotional, the competencies and capabilities required to manage change focus on affecting instinctive human reactions. Gartner has identified five key elements, when appropriately employed, which can radically improve enterprise change results. Conversely, any single element, if unaddressed, will greatly diminish probabilities for success. The five key elements are:

1. The imperative, which is the case for change. In the case of our approach to IT benefits realization this can be positively projected as an opportunity to once and for all derive business value from IT while clarifying everyone's roles and responsibilities and clear objectives, in an environment of learning, not blame.

231

2. Leaders, who possess a vision of the future, and instigate and sustain change to meet this vision.

3. Levers, which are the tools change leaders employ to encourage desired behaviors and achieve required outcomes.

4. Affected agents, the people who must support and adapt to the change initiative.

5. Stabilizers, which are organizational strengths deployed as stabilizing forces or sources of confidence. The most important leadership competencies are those required to deploy these elements effectively.

The planning for change management must include stakeholder management activities with clear processes, schedules, resources and responsibilities. Communication should include listening and feedback. It should continually reinforce leadership's vision for the future and the business imperative driving the change. Messages should describe what will be different and clarify leaders' expectations. New competencies, responsibilities, behaviors, and help for employees to transition should be discussed. Success of stakeholder management should be continually reviewed and tactical adjustments made quickly. Those who have committed to the change should be used to encourage others. Consistent, sustained leadership support for the chosen levers is crucial as stakeholder pressure is increased. Communication is critical to persuading affected stakeholders of the change imperative, of management's commitment to change, and of the probability for success. Without communication, those affected cannot understand the change initiative's personal implications. Without understanding, they will never adapt. Ultimately, everyone affected should be able to answer the question, "What's in it for me?" So consciously build project momentum through increasing pressures and rewards, communication, and leadership visibility. Build a formal, ongoing communication strategy into the change initiative project plan.

Finally, bear in mind that change is hard, painful and expensive. Even when a change initiative's ultimate impact is positive, as this will be, those affected by it often resist. Widespread expectations of discomfort combined with an almost primal fear of the unknown persistently cause change initiatives to fail. Intuitively, most business leaders understand this, but they fail to adequately address the problem. Few organizations provide their leadership with formal change management training or accompany major change initiatives with institutionalized management processes. As a result, change occurs haphazardly, is often too little too late, and is achieved only with tremendous organizational pain. So ideally you should develop change competencies within your organization before implementing the Gartner benefits realization framework.

Through 2008, market, technology and financial discontinuities will materially increase as a result of e-business-induced change. Organizational inability to manage these discontinuities will result in a 30 percent increase in the failure of major business/IT initiatives (0.7 probability).

Terms like "Internet years" and "zero latency" are entering the management vernacular. Magazines with titles like Fast Company have become popular business periodicals. These are potent indications that rates of change are accelerating beyond anything previously experienced, that the pace is both pushed and enabled by IT, and that change competencies are a required survival skill.

Conceptual Framework: The Change Absorption Framework (see Figure I.1) captures the essence of change as a potentially infinite flow, and the ability of people to absorb it as a finite stock. The tension of this relationship—the incongruity between the flow of change and the human capability to absorb it—is a fundamental cause of change initiative failure.

■ THE HUMAN RESPONSE TO CHANGE

Paralyzation from change is the human equivalent of overloaded circuits. It is analogous to a power outage on an exceptionally hot day. As more and more air conditioners come online, demand for power begins to approach capacity limits, increasingly stressing the system. As stress on the system

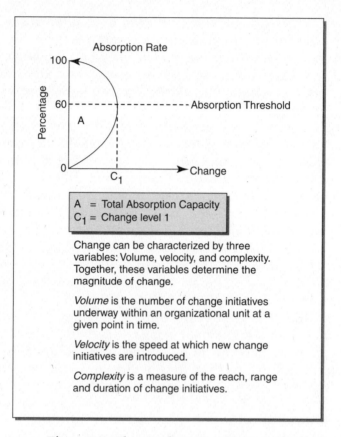

Absorption Rate

Percentage

100

60 ------------------------------ Absorption Threshold

A

0

C₁

Change

A = Total Absorption Capacity
C₁ = Change level 1

Change can be characterized by three variables: Volume, velocity, and complexity. Together, these variables determine the magnitude of change.

Volume is the number of change initiatives underway within an organizational unit at a given point in time.

Velocity is the speed at which new change initiatives are introduced.

Complexity is a measure of the reach, range and duration of change initiatives.

Figure I.1   Change Absorption Framework

grows, system performance begins to decline. The lights begin to flicker; at 100 percent utilization, they go out completely. The human response to change-induced stress is poorer and poorer performance, which, unless managed, can culminate in complete shutdown. This response is reflected in the reverse curve of the Change Absorption Framework.

Beyond the absorption threshold, additional change initiatives become counterproductive. The theoretical change absorption capacity of an individual or group of individuals may be 100 percent, but at some lesser utilization level, overall performance degrades until people are paralyzed by the endless barrage. When this occurs, absorption capacity is effectively reduced to zero.

Key Issues: Given the profound implication of institutional willingness and ability to change on the success of strategic initiatives, the Gartner approach focuses on four Key Issues, as follows:

1. **How will enterprises develop an understanding of their current capacity for change?**

   Understanding the enterprise's current change capacity is the first step in developing a change management strategy, since it drives how many change initiatives can be undertaken at any given time and how fast they can be implemented. Change capacity is defined by employee willingness and ability to change. It is affected by organizational history and culture, leadership credibility, attitudes and trust toward management, perceptions of urgency, employee skills, and a collective experience of change. The Gartner approach focuses on assessing the enterprise's capacity for change as part of a broader focus on improving the enterprise's change management competencies and success rates (see Figure I.1).

2. **How will enterprises accurately assess the scope and impact of a change initiative?**

   Accurately assessing the scope of change and the capacity of an organization to absorb it in the context of other initiatives is among the most difficult tasks in a change management process. Underestimation of either scope or capacity inevitably leads to cost and schedule overruns or, in the worst case, total collapse of the change initiative. Depending on the criticality of the change initiative, such problems can be catastrophic. The Gartner approach focuses on conducting scope assessment and predicting gaps in change capacity or organizational readiness (see Figure I.2).

3. **How will enterprises increase their capacity for change?**

   Some organizations are better at managing and absorbing change than others. Enterprises facing exceptionally

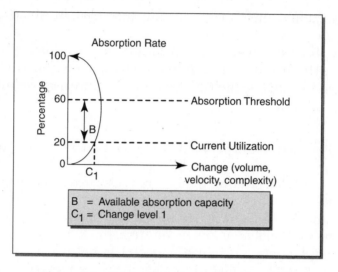

Figure I.2 Raising the Absorption Threshold

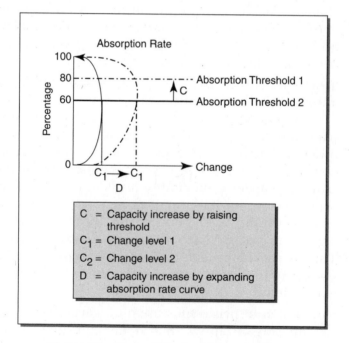

Figure I.3 Expanding the Absorption Curve

nimble competitors must not only improve their change management competencies, but increase the organization's overall capacity for change. The Gartner approach is to identify the strategic options for improving the enterprise's change profile by focusing on techniques for influencing employee willingness and ability to change (Figure I.3).

4. How will enterprises ration, orchestrate, and manage change to improve strategy execution?

Change is a process, and as a process, it can be managed. Our consultancy provides insights developed through the Change Absorption Framework, as well as the experiences of best-in-class organizations, to identify critical success factors, best practices and methodologies for instituting change.

Appendix J

Financial Metrics

Payback Period is a very simple measure, addressing the length of time it takes to recover the original investment. If an investment of $5,000 generates benefits worth $2,000 per annum, the Payback Period is 2.5 years.

■ NET PRESENT VALUE (NPV)

In the context of NPV calculations, net value refers to the total benefits of the investment minus the costs, represented in terms of today's values. To refer to the present value of a project is to say that the values have been subjected to discounting, that is, an interest rate reflecting the anticipated cost of money has been applied to the costs and benefits. This means that net benefit with a current value of $1,000 might have a value of $900 if achieved next year, and $800 if achieved the year after that. And again, this is as it should be.

■ INTERNAL RATE OF RETURN (IRR)

The internal rate of return, sometimes referred to as the discounted cash-flow return (DCFR), represents the interest rate at which the NPV is 0, that is, it measures the actual percentage rate of return the project will achieve. Many companies have what is known as a "hurdle rate" which is the minimum rate of return.

➤ Optimizing the Use of NPV and IRR in Evaluating IT Projects

There are several ways of looking at this issue.

The crude Payback Period measures the length of time it takes to recover the investment. Depending on the particular circumstances of a company, this could be the most critical condition. It is certainly an important consideration, and as shown, can be refined by using the system to discount the cash flows, and by basing the Payback Period on the capital cost of the project. Nonetheless, used in isolation, the Payback Period does not address either the amount of profit from the project or the real rate of return. Once a project's net cash flows have been discounted, the NPV measures the profit generated in terms of present values. In other words it measures it in absolute cash terms.

➤ The IRR (DCFR) on the Other Hand Measures a Percentage Rate of Return

So the Payback Period measures the time it takes to recover the investment, the NPV represents the amount of money at present values a project will earn, and the IRR measures the effectiveness of the use to which the original capital was put (i.e., the rate of return). For a single project therefore, both NPV and IRR will give the same answer as to whether a project is viable or not, because if the NPV is positive, it must have an IRR greater than the discount rate used in calculating the NPV.

Assuming a choice of projects, an unlimited supply of capital and other resources to undertake all the projects on hand, it is valid to select all projects with a positive NPV. The same result would be achieved by selecting all projects with an IRR greater than the discount rate used in calculating NPVs.

In the more realistic situation of inadequate resources for all the projects available, the most effective use of capital must be sought. This is done by obtaining the IRR for each project, and ranking them in order of return. Starting from the one with the highest return, each project is selected until available capital is used up.

The value Payback Period, NPV, and IRR analyzes should not be overstated merely because they appear to demonstrate precision. They should be seen as a useful tool when forecasting the anticipated monetary impact of the investment, but no more.

Enterprises with advanced management techniques seek to look behind and beyond financial measures such as those used in CBA and connect business objectives to the behaviors, tactics, and actions that enterprise stakeholders and employees pursue to meet these financial measures. Essentially, IT should crystallize the cause-and-effect relationship between adherence to strategic objectives, financial performance, and excellence in internal business processes in a context where the chances of achieving the potential benefits are maximized.

Index